GCSE AQA
Extension Science
The Workbook

This book is for anyone doing **GCSE AQA Extension Science**.

It's full of **tricky questions**... each one designed to make you **sweat** — because that's the only way you'll get any **better**.

There are questions to see **what facts** you know. There are questions to see how well you can **apply those facts**. And there are questions to see what you know about **how science works**.

It's also got some daft bits in to try and make the whole experience at least vaguely entertaining for you.

What CGP is all about

Our sole aim here at CGP is to produce the highest quality books — carefully written, immaculately presented and dangerously close to being funny.

Then we work our socks off to get them out to you — at the cheapest possible prices.

Contents

Biology 3a — Life Processes

Biology 3b — Humans and Their Environment

Chemistry 3a — Elements, Water and Organic Chemistry

Chemistry 3b — Titrations, Energy and Chemical Tests

Physics 3a — Medical Applications of Physics

Physics 3b — Forces and Electromagnetism

Published by CGP

Editors:
Charlotte Burrows, Katherine Craig, Mary Falkner, Felicity Inkpen, Rosie McCurrie, Jane Sawers, Sarah Williams.

Contributors:
Michael Aiken, Steve Coggins, Mike Dagless, Jane Davies, Max Fishel, James Foster, Paddy Gannon, Dr Iona MJ Hamilton, Barbara Mascetti.

ISBN: 978 1 84762 854 1

With thanks to Janet Cruse-Sawyer, Mark A Edwards, Ben Fletcher, Jamie Sinclair and Karen Wells for the proofreading.
With thanks to Jan Greenway, Laura Jakubowski and Laura Stoney for the copyright research.

Data on page 31, source ww2.defra.gov.uk © Crown copyright reproduced under the terms of the Click-Use licence.

Table of Kidney Failure Statistics on page 18 reproduced with permission from the NHS UK Transplant. www.organdonation.nhs.uk

Graph of average surface temperature of Earth on page 32 © Crown copyright 2006, The Met Office.

With thanks to the Intergovernmental Panel on Climate Change for permission to reproduce the graph of atmospheric gas concentrations used on page 32.

Every effort has been made to locate copyright holders and obtain permission to reproduce sources. For those sources where it has been difficult to trace the originator of the work, we would be grateful for information. If any copyright holder would like us to make an amendment to the acknowledgements, please notify us and we will gladly update the book at the next reprint.
Thank you.

Groovy website: www.cgpbooks.co.uk

Printed by Elanders Ltd, Newcastle upon Tyne.
Jolly bits of clipart from CorelDRAW®
Based on the classic CGP style created by Richard Parsons.

Osmosis

Q1 This diagram shows a tank separated into two by a partially permeable membrane.

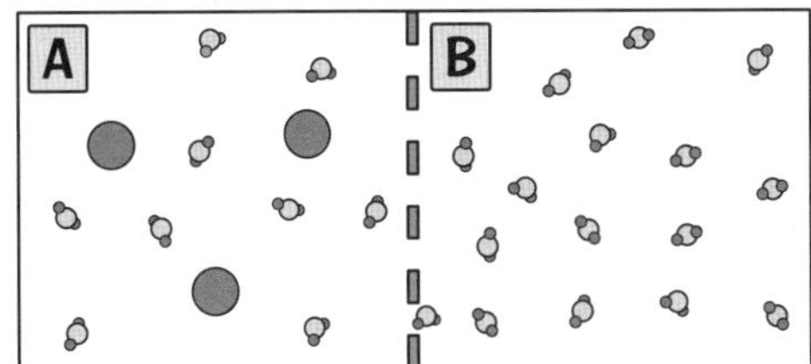

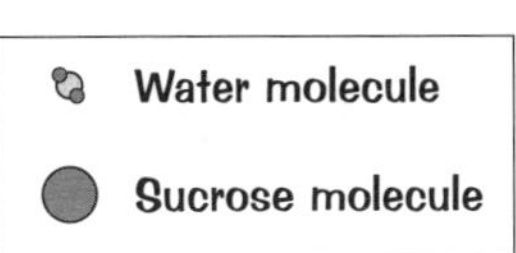

a) On which side of the membrane is there the higher concentration of water molecules?

.....B.....

b) In which direction would you expect more water molecules to travel — from A to B or from B to A?

.....B to A.....

c) Predict whether the level of liquid on side B will **rise** or **fall**. Explain your answer.

The liquid level on side B will .....fall....., **because** .....more water molecules would pass through the paricable permuable membrane.....

Q2 Some **potato cylinders** were placed in solutions of different **salt concentrations**. At the start of the experiment each cylinder was 50 mm long. Their final lengths are recorded in the table below.

Concentration of salt (molar)	Final length of potato cylinder (mm)	Change in length of potato cylinder (mm)
0	60	
0.25	58	
0.5	56	
0.75	70	
1	50	
1.25	45	

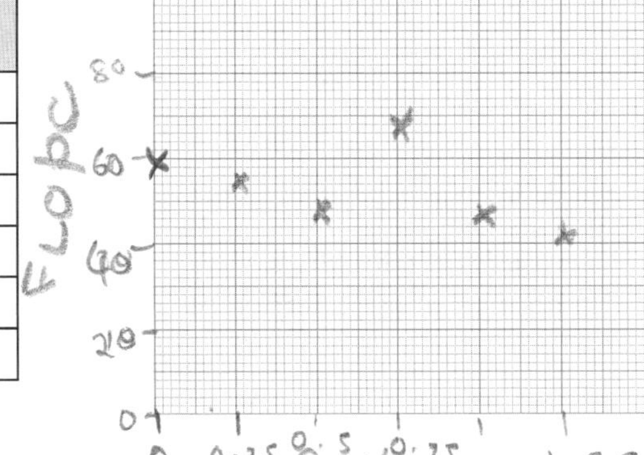

a) Plot the points for concentration of salt solution vs final length of potato cylinders on the grid.

b) Work out the change in length of each of the cylinders and complete the table above.

c) Study the pattern of the results.

i) State the salt concentration(s) that produced unexpected results. ....

ii) Suggest a method for deciding which of the results are correct.

....

d) State three factors that should have been kept constant to ensure this was a fair test.

....

....

....

Osmosis

Q3 The diagram below shows some **body cells** bathed in **tissue fluid**. A blood vessel flows close to the cells, providing water. The cells shown have a low concentration of water inside them.

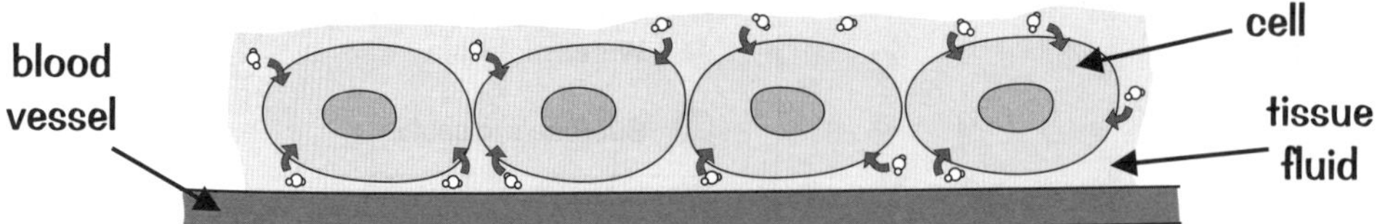

a) Is the concentration of water higher in the **tissue fluid** or inside the **cells**?

tissue fluid

b) In which direction would you expect more water to travel — **into** the cells or **out of** the cells? Explain your answer.

into the cell since the water is travelling from a higher concentration (tissue fluid) to a lower concentration.

c) Explain why osmosis appears to stop after a while.

the concentrations become equal.

Q4 Joan was making a meal of **salted ham** and **fruit salad**. She covered the meat in water and left it to soak for a few hours. When she returned, the meat was much bigger in size.

a) Use the term **osmosis** to help you explain the change in appearance of the ham.

the water has moved from a higher concentration to a lower concentration through osmosis.

b) To make her fruit salad, Joan cut up some oranges and apples, sprinkled sugar over them and left them overnight. When she examined the fruit next morning it was surrounded by a **liquid**.

i) Suggest what the liquid might be. fruit juice.

ii) Explain where the liquid has come from.

the fruits.

iii) Joan washed some raisins and sultanas to add to her salad. She observed that they became swollen. Explain what has happened this time.

Gas and Solute Exchange

Q1 Substances move through partially permeable membranes by **three** processes.

a) Place a cross in the correct boxes to identify the features of each process.

Feature	Diffusion	Osmosis	Active transport
Substances move from areas of higher concentration to areas of lower concentration			
Requires energy			

b) What is the main difference between diffusion and osmosis?

....

Q2 Indicate whether each of the following statements is **true** or **false**.

		True	False
a)	Leaves are adapted to aid the diffusion of gases.		
b)	Guard cells are important for controlling water loss from leaves.		
c)	In dry conditions leaf stomata are likely to be open.		
d)	Air spaces in leaves reduce the surface area for gas exchange.		
e)	Plants are likely to wilt when they lose more water than is replaced.		
f)	Plants mainly lose water from their roots.		

Q3 A diagram of a cross-section through part of a **leaf** is shown.

a) Suggest what substance is represented by each of the letters shown on the diagram.

A ....

B ....

C ....

b) By what process do all these substances enter and leave the leaf? ....

c) How is the amount of these substances that enter and leave the leaf controlled?

....

....

d) State two places where gaseous exchange takes place in a leaf.

1. ....

2. ....

e) Suggest one advantage of leaves having a flattened shape.

....

Gas and Solute Exchange

Q4 Circle the correct word(s) from each pair to complete the passage below.

In life processes, **gases** / **solids** and **dissolved** / **undissolved** substances have to move through an exchange surface to get to where they're needed. Exchange surfaces are adapted to **maximise** / **minimise** effectiveness. For example, they are **thick** / **thin** so substances only have a **short** / **long** distance to diffuse. They have a **small** / **large** surface area so lots of a substance can diffuse at once. Exchange surfaces in animals have lots of blood vessels to get stuff into and out of the **blood** / **stomach** quickly. Gas exchange surfaces in animals are often **oily** / **ventilated** too. Exchanging substances gets more difficult in **smaller** / **bigger** and more **simple** / **complex** organisms — the place where the substances are needed is a **short** / **long** way away from exchange surfaces.

Q5 Lucy was investigating the water loss from basil plants in **different conditions**. She used twelve plants, three plants in each of the four different conditions. The plants were weighed before and after the experiment. She calculated the % change in the mass and recorded her results in a table.

a) Calculate the average % change in plant mass for the three plants in each of the conditions and write the results in the table.

Plant	In a room (% change in mass)	Next to a fan (% change in mass)	By a lamp (% change in mass)	Next to a fan and by a lamp (% change in mass)
1	5	8	10	13
2	5	9	11	15
3	4	11	9	13
Average				

b) Which conditions caused the greatest water loss? Circle the correct answer.

in a room　　next to a fan　　by a lamp　　next to a fan and by a lamp

c) Suggest why Lucy used **three** plants in each of the conditions shown.

....

d) Lucy then covered the lower surfaces of the leaves with **petroleum jelly**. Explain how this would affect the rate of water loss from the leaves.

Petroleum jelly is a waterproof substance.

....

....

e) The water loss from a plant in a hot, dry day is shown on the graph. Sketch the graph you would expect for the same plant on a **cold**, **wet** day.

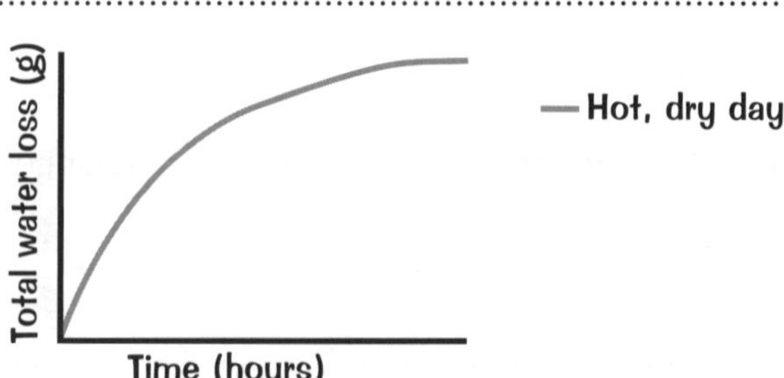

Top Tips: Diffusion, osmosis and active transport... or 'how stuff gets from one place to another' if you like. Remember, active transport is the odd one out — it's **active** so it needs **energy**.

The Breathing System

Q1 **Ventilation** involves the breathing system.

a) Define **ventilation**.

....

b) Explain why ventilation is needed.

....

....

Q2 a) On the diagram show the positions of the following structures by placing the correct letter in the correct box:

A	alveolus	**D**	bronchiole
B	bronchus	**E**	ribcage
C	trachea	**F**	diaphragm

b) Complete the passages below using the words given. Each word may be used more than once.

out	**flattens**	**drawn into**	**in**		
diaphragm	**increases**	**decreases**	**down**	**intercostal**	**up**
forced out of	**rises**	**volume**	**relax**	**ribcage**	**fall**

i) When we breathe .... the .... muscles and the .... contract. This means the diaphragm .... and the ribcage and the sternum move .... and .... This makes the volume of the thorax .... in size, which causes a .... in pressure. Air is then .... the lungs.

ii) Breathing out occurs when the intercostal muscles and the diaphragm .... This means that the .... and sternum move .... and .... As a result the .... of the thorax .... and the pressure ...., meaning that air is .... the lungs.

Q3 a) What is an **artificial ventilator**?

....

b) Explain how a modern artificial ventilator works.

....

....

Diffusion Through Cell Membranes

Q1 Parts of the human body are **adapted** to speed up the **rate of diffusion** of various substances.

a) State **two** parts of the body that are adapted to aid diffusion.

....

b) Name **two** substances that enter the bloodstream by diffusion.

....

Q2 The movements of two gases **A** and **B** in an **alveolus** are shown.

a) Add these labels to the diagram: **capillary**, **plasma**, **red blood cell**, **alveolus**.

b) Name the two gases that are passing through the walls of the alveolus.

A ....

B ....

c) Name the **process** by which these gases travel across the wall of the alveolus.

....

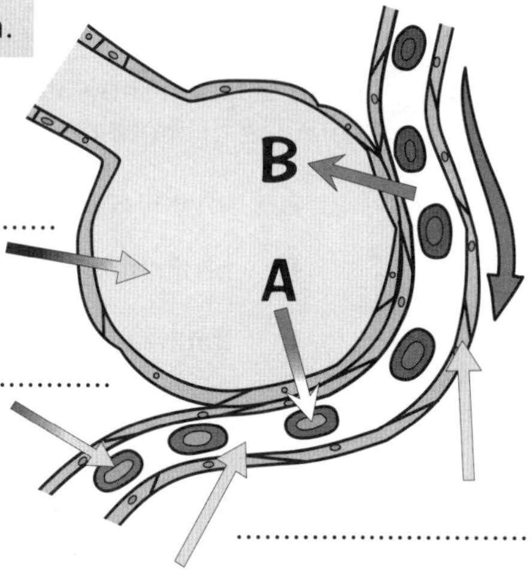

B

A

Q3 Villi increase the **surface area** of the gut for the uptake of nutrients. Pablo conducted an experiment to investigate the effect of surface area using four **gelatine cubes** of **different sizes**. He placed the cubes in a dish of food dye and measured how quickly they absorbed the dye. His results are shown in the table.

Size (cm)	Surface area (cm^2)	Time taken for dye uptake (s)
1 x 1 x 1		41.6
2 x 2 x 2		9.3
5 x 5 x 5		1.7
10 x 10 x 10		0.4

a) Calculate the missing values for **surface area**.

b) Complete these statements by circling the correct word.

i) As the cubes become bigger in size their surface area becomes **bigger** / **smaller**.

ii) As the surface area becomes bigger the rate of dye uptake **increases** / **decreases**.

c) Explain how the results from this experiment show that villi increase the rate of nutrient uptake from the gut.

....

....

d) Give **one** other feature of villi that helps to speed up the uptake of nutrients. ....

Active Transport

Q1 Tick the boxes to show whether the following statements are **true** or **false**.

		True	False
a)	Active transport allows cells to absorb ions from very concentrated solutions.	☐	☐
b)	Active transport allows substances to be taken up against the concentration gradient.	☐	☐
c)	Dissolved substances in the gut move into the blood by active transport.	☐	☐

Q2 A diagram of a **specialised plant cell** is shown.

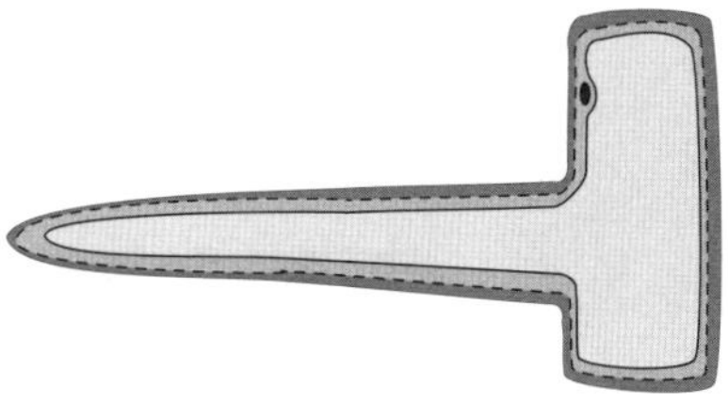

a) Name the type of cell shown. ....

b) What is the main **function** of this type of cell?

....

c) Explain why minerals are **not** usually absorbed from the soil by the process of **diffusion**.

....

....

d) Explain how these specialised cells absorb minerals from the soil.
Use the words **active transport**, **concentration**, **respiration** and **energy** in your answer.

....

....

Q3 Two germinating barley seedlings were placed in solutions that contained a known concentration of **potassium ions**, as shown in the diagram. The uptake of potassium ions was measured.

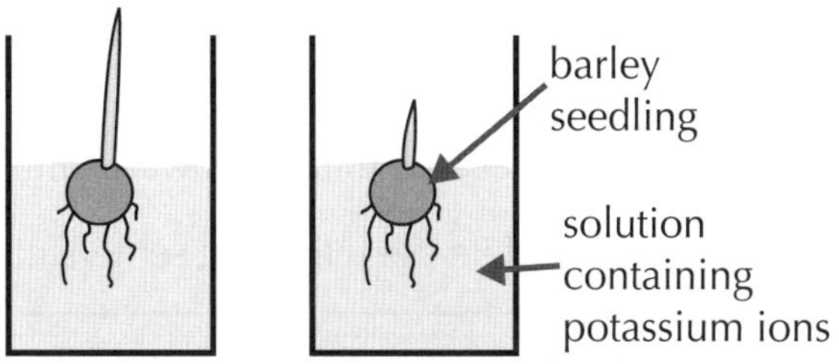

barley seedling

solution containing potassium ions

Seedling A

Seedling B

a) State **two** ways to ensure this is a fair test.

....

....

The graph below shows the uptake of potassium ions by the barley seedlings.

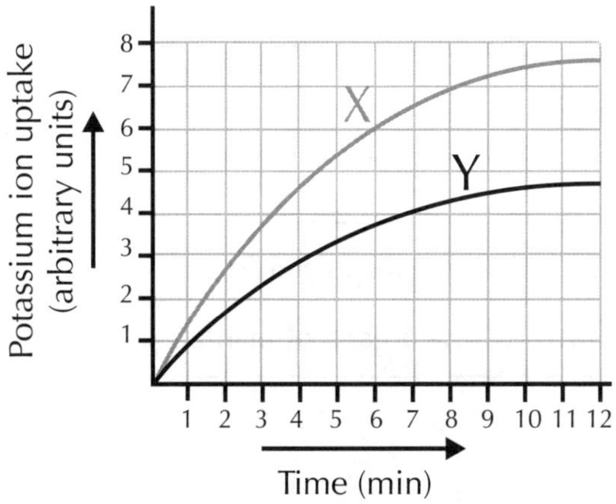

Potassium ion uptake (arbitrary units)

X

Y

Time (min)

b) Which curve represents seedling **A**?
Circle the correct answer.

X **Y**

Explain how you decided.

....

....

c) What is the potassium ion uptake for seedling A after **10 minutes**? ....

Water Flow Through Plants

Q1 Complete this diagram of a **plant** according to the instructions given below.

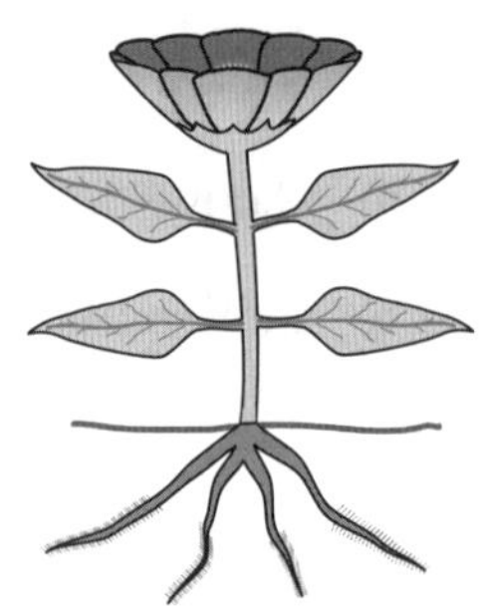

a) Put an **X** on the diagram to show one place where water enters the plant.

b) Add a **Y** to the diagram to show one place where water leaves the plant.

c) Add arrows to the diagram to show how water moves from where it enters to where it leaves.

Q2 Choose from the following words to complete the passage.

Each word can only be used once.

osmosis leaves evaporation roots flowers leaf diffusion transpiration stream xylem

Most water leaves plants through the .... by the processes of .... and .... This creates a slight shortage of water in the ...., which draws water from the rest of the plant through the .... vessels. This causes more water to be drawn up from the ...., and so there's a constant .... of water through the plant.

Q3 Flowering plants have **separate transport systems**.

a) Name the **two** types of transport tissue in flowering plants.

1. .... 2. ....

b) i) Which tissue transports water and minerals? ....

ii) Complete the following sentence:

Water and minerals are transported from the .... of the plants to the .... and ....

c) i) Which tissue carries dissolved sugars? ....

ii) Complete the following sentence:

Dissolved sugars are made in the .... and transported to the .... regions and .... organs of plants.

Circulatory System — The Heart

Q1 Tick the boxes to show whether the following statements about the **heart** are **true** or **false**.

		True	False
a)	The heart is a tissue.	☐	☐
b)	The heart pumps blood around the body.	☐	☐
c)	The walls of the heart are mostly made of muscle tissue.	☐	☐
d)	The heart has two main chambers.	☐	☐

Q2 The diagram below shows the human **heart**, as seen from the front. The left atrium has been labelled. Complete the remaining labels **a)** to **h)**.

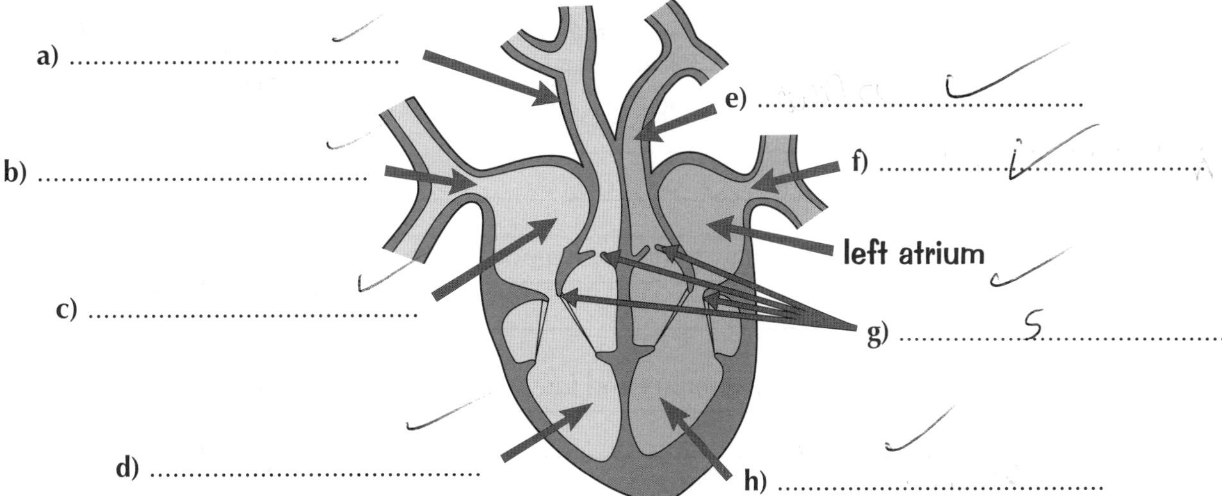

i) What is the function of the valves in the heart and in veins?

....

j) Use the words given to fill in the blanks in the paragraph below.

vein heart deoxygenated lungs artery oxygenated double

Humans have a .... circulatory system. In the first circuit, blood is pumped from the .... to the .... In the second circuit, ... blood leaves the heart and goes around to body and .... blood returns to the heart.

Top Tips: Make sure that you can label all the bits of the heart and the blood vessels, and that you understand exactly where the blood goes. Remember, **a**rteries carry blood **a**way from the heart.

Circulatory System — The Heart

Q3 State two **functions** of the circulation system. For each function you have given name **two substances** that are **transported**.

Function 1: ....

substances transported: .... and ....

Function 2: ....

substances transported: .... and ....

Q4 Put the words below in the boxes to show the correct sequence of **blood flow** around the body. Each word may be used more than once. The first one has been done for you.

arteries **ventricles** **atria** **veins** **out** **organs**

Blood enters the ....atria......... of the heart.

The .... contract and force blood into the ....

The .... contract and force blood .... of the heart.

Blood flows from the heart to .... through ....

Blood returns to the heart through ....

Q5 The diagram shows the **blood vessels** of the **heart**.

Write the name of each blood vessel beside the letters on the diagram.

A .... B ....

C .... D ....

Right-hand side Left-hand side

Circulatory System — Blood Vessels

Q1 A diagram of a **capillary** is shown.

a) Capillary walls are only **one cell** thick.
How does this feature make them suited to their function?

They are only one cell thick
This increases the rate of diffusion by decreasing the distance over which it occurs

b) Name **two gases** that diffuse through the walls of capillaries.

CO_2 and oxygen

c) Name **one** other substance that diffuses through the walls of capillaries.

~~food~~ urea

Q2 The pictures below show cross sections of two **blood vessels** — an artery and a vein.

A B

a) Which blood vessel is an artery and which a vein?

A = Artery B = vein

b) Explain how the following structures are related to the **function** of the blood vessel.

i) Muscular and elastic walls of arteries Strong to withstand pressure from the heart

ii) Valves in veins keeps low pressure blood flowing back to heart

Q3 Gareth did an experiment to compare the elasticity of **arteries** and **veins**. He dissected out an artery and a vein from a piece of fresh meat. He then took a 5 cm length of each vessel, hung different masses on it, and measured how much it stretched. His results are shown in the table.

mass added (g)	length of blood vessel (mm)	
	artery	vein
0	50	50
5	51	53
10	53	56
15	55	59
20	56	-

a) Suggest one way in which Gareth could tell which was the artery and which was the vein when he was dissecting the meat.

~~The veins would~~ ~~The ve~~
The artery would withhold more pressure by the mass added

b) If Gareth plots his results on a graph, which variable should he put on the vertical axis, and why?

lenghr of blood vessel

c) Which vessel stretched more easily? Explain why this was.

vein because the walls aren thick

d) Why did he take both vessels from the same piece of meat?

So they have ~~so~~ some common propertius

Circulatory System — The Blood

Q1 Which of these statements are **true**, and which are **false**? Tick the correct boxes.

	Statement	True	False
a)	The function of red blood cells is to fight germs.		
b)	White blood cells have no nucleus.		
c)	The liquid part of blood is called urine.		
d)	Platelets are small fragments of cells.		
e)	Platelets help seal wounds to prevent blood loss.		
f)	Platelets have a nucleus.		
g)	Blood is a tissue.		

Tissues are made of groups of similar cells.

Q2 **Red blood cells** carry **oxygen** in the blood.

a) **i)** Name the substance in red blood cells that combines with oxygen. ....

ii) Name the substance created when oxygen joins with this substance. ....

b) Red blood cells are replaced about every 120 days. Approximately how many times per year are all the red cells in the body replaced? ....

Q3 **White blood cells** defend the body against **disease**.

State three ways in which white blood cells can protect your body from microorganisms.

1. ....

2. ....

3. ....

Q4 a) List six things that are carried by **plasma**.

1. ....
2. ....
3. ....
4. ....
5. ....
6. ....

b) For each of the substances listed in the table, state where each is travelling **from** and **to** in the blood.

Substance	Travelling from	Travelling to
Urea		
Carbon dioxide		
Glucose		

Circulation Aids

Q1 Complete the passage using the words provided below.

heart attack narrow beating irritate open tubes clotting muscles arteries scar tissue coronary

Stents are .... that can be inserted inside coronary .... that have become too .... Stents keep them ...., making sure blood can pass through to the heart .... This keeps the person's heart .... Stents are a way of lowering the risk of a .... in a person with .... heart disease. But over time, the artery can narrow again as stents can .... the artery and make .... grow. The patient also has to take drugs to stop blood .... on the stent.

Q2 Read the descriptions of the following patients before choosing a suitable treatment (A, B, C or D) from the list.

A — artificial heart transplant

B — artificial replacement valve

C — artificial blood product

D — stent

a) Annie has been involved in an accident and has lost a lot of blood. ☐

b) Alistair has been diagnosed with a blocked artery to the heart muscle. ☐

c) Clive has a damaged heart valve. He is known to react badly to the drugs that are normally used to suppress the immune system. ☐

d) Valerie is a 40 year old woman, who has a badly diseased heart. She is in danger of dying very soon if she is not treated. ☐

Q3 Artificial hearts are mechanical devices that can pump a person's blood if their heart fails.

a) Other than keeping them alive, give **one** advantage to a patient of receiving an artificial heart.

....

b) Give **two** disadvantages to a patient of receiving an artificial heart.

....

....

Top Tips: You might be asked to evaluate artificial replacements in your exam — don't panic, look at any information given and use your knowledge of the pros and cons to write your answer.

Homeostasis

Q1 Define the word '**homeostasis**'.

....

Q2 **Waste products** have to be removed from the body.

a) How is carbon dioxide removed from the body?

....

b) Other than carbon dioxide, name one waste product that the body needs to remove.

....

Q3 The human body needs to be kept at a temperature of around **37 °C**.

a) Explain how your body **monitors** its internal temperature.

....

....

b) How does the body receive information about skin temperature?

....

Q4 a) Fill in this table describing how different parts of the body help to bring your body temperature back to normal if you get **too hot** or **too cold**. One has been done for you.

	Too hot	Too cold
hair	**Hairs lie down flat**	
sweat glands		
blood vessels		

b) Describe how **shivering** helps to warm the body when it's cold.

....

....

The Kidneys and Homeostasis

Q1 Tick the correct boxes to show whether these sentences are **true** or **false**.

		True	False
a)	The kidneys make urea.	☐	☐
b)	Breaking down excess amino acids produces urea.	☐	☐
c)	The liver makes urea.	☐	☐
d)	The kidneys monitor blood temperature.	☐	☐
e)	The bladder stores urine.	☐	☐

Q2 One of the kidney's roles is to adjust the **ion content** of the **blood**.

a) Where do the ions in the body come from?

....

b) What would happen if the ion content of the blood wasn't controlled?

....

....

Q3 The kidneys are involved in the control of the body's **water levels**.

Complete the table showing how your body maintains a water balance on hot and cold days.

	Do you sweat **a lot** or **a little**?	Is the amount of urine you produce **high** or **low**?	Is the urine you produce **more** or **less** concentrated?
Hot Day			
Cold Day			

Q4 You can replace lost water during exercise by consuming a **sports drink**.

a) **i)** Apart from water, name **two** substances that sports drinks usually contain.

1. .... 2. ....

ii) For each of the substances you named in part **a) i)**, explain their function in a sports drink.

....

....

b) Some sports drink manufacturers claim that their drink will rehydrate you faster than water. Suggest **one** thing you need to look out for when deciding whether the claim is true or not.

....

Kidney Function

Q1 The diagram shows the steps that occur from the entry of blood into the kidneys to the exit of blood from the kidneys. Write the labels **A** to **G** in the diagram to show the correct order.

A Wastes such as urea, are carried out of the nephron to the bladder, whilst reabsorbed materials leave the kidneys in the renal vein.

B Small molecules are squeezed into the Bowman's capsule. Large molecules remain in the blood.

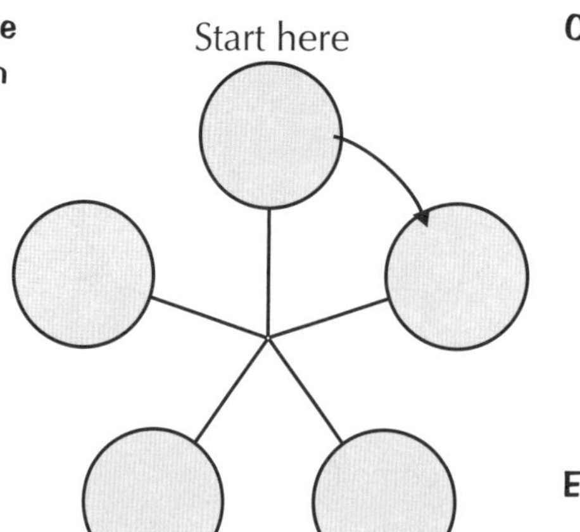

C Useful products are reabsorbed from the nephron and enter the capillaries.

D Molecules travel from the Bowman's capsule along the nephron.

E Blood enters the kidney through the renal artery.

Q2 The blood entering the kidney contains the following:

ions water proteins sugar urea blood cells

a) List the things that are:

i) filtered out of the blood ....

ii) reabsorbed ....

iii) released in the urine ....

b) Which process is responsible for the **reabsorption** of each substance you have listed above?

c) i) Name two things that do **not** enter the Bowman's capsule.

....

ii) Explain why these things are not able to leave the bloodstream.

....

Q3 Three people are tested to see how healthy their kidneys are. Levels of **protein** and **glucose** in their urine are measured. The results are shown in the table.

Which of the three subjects might have kidney damage? Explain how you decided.

....

....

....

Subject	Protein (mg/24 hours)	Glucose (mmol/litre)
1	12	0
2	260	1.0
3	0	0

Kidney Failure

Q1 **Kidney failure** can be treated by dialysis or a kidney transplant. Place a tick in the table to show the features of the two types of treatment.

Feature of treatment	Dialysis	Transplant
High risk of infection		
Long-term, one-off treatment		
Patient can lead a relatively normal life		
Patient must take drugs		
Patient usually needs to live near a hospital		

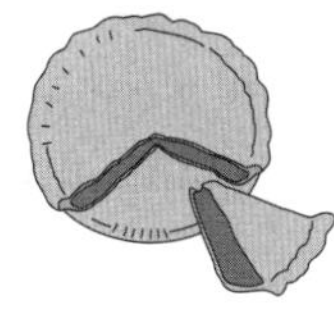

Q2 A model of **dialysis** is shown below. No movement of substances has taken place yet.

Blood | Dialysis fluid

membrane

Red blood cell
Protein
Urea
Water
Glucose

a) **i)** Which two substances will **not** diffuse across the membrane from the bloodstream into the dialysis fluid.

....

ii) Explain your answer.

....

....

b) Which substance's concentration will increase in the dialysis fluid? ....

c) What do you notice about the concentration of glucose on either side of the membrane? Suggest a reason for this.

....

....

Q3 A donor kidney can be **rejected** by a patient's immune system.

a) Explain why a patient's antibodies may attack the antigens on a donor kidney.

....

b) List **two** steps that are taken to reduce the chances of rejection of a transplanted kidney.

1. ....

2. ....

Kidney Failure

Q4 One method of treatment for kidney failure is to use **dialysis**.

a) The steps in dialysis are listed. Number the steps in the correct order by writing 1 to 5 in the boxes.

☐ Excess water, ions and wastes are filtered out of the blood and pass into the dialysis fluid.

☐ The patient's blood flows into the dialysis machine and between partially permeable membranes that are surrounded by dialysis fluid.

☐ Blood is returned to the patient's body using a vein in their arm.

☐ Dialysis continues until nearly all the waste and excess substances are removed.

☐ A needle is inserted into a blood vessel in the patient's arm to remove blood.

b) Explain why it is important that the dialysis fluid has the same concentration of dissolved ions as healthy blood.

....

c) Why does dialysis need to be done regularly?

....

Q5 The table shows the number of UK patients with **kidney failure** in **2004** and predicted numbers for **2013**.

	Year	
	2004	**2013**
Total number of patients with kidney failure	37 000	68 000
Number receiving dialysis	20 500	
Number that have received a transplant		30 000

a) Calculate the number of patients who received a kidney **transplant** in **2004**. Write your answer in the table.

b) Calculate the number of patients who are likely to be receiving **dialysis** in **2013**. Write your answer in the table.

c) This table shows the cost of each treatment.

Treatment	**Average cost per patient (£)**
Dialysis	30 000 per year
Transplant	20 000
Anti-rejection drugs	6 500 per year

Calculate the amount of money saved per patient when a **transplant** is performed:

i) instead of **one** year of **dialysis**.

....

ii) instead of **three** years of **dialysis**.

....

....

Don't forget that transplant patients need drugs to stop organ rejection.

Top Tips: Kidneys do loads of important jobs and that's why kidney failure is so dangerous. You can live with only one kidney though — so it's possible for some people with kidney failure to receive a donated kidney from a member of their family or from another suitable donor.

Controlling Blood Glucose

Q1 Most people's **blood sugar** level is controlled as part of **homeostasis**.

a) Where does the **sugar** in your blood come from?

....

b) Name **one organ** that is involved in the control of blood sugar level.

....

c) Name **two hormones** involved in the regulation of blood sugar level.

....

Q2 Complete the flow chart to show what happens when the **glucose** level in the blood gets too **high**.

Blood contains too much glucose.

↘

.... is released by the ....

↘

.... makes the .... store glucose. Excess blood glucose is converted to ....

↘

.... is removed from the ....

↘

Blood glucose level is now ....

Q3 Explain how the blood sugar level is controlled when there is **not enough** glucose in the blood.

....

....

....

Controlling Blood Glucose

Q4 Ruby and Paul both have **type 1 diabetes**, so they need to **control** their glucose levels carefully.

a) Explain what type 1 diabetes is.

....

....

b) Describe **three** ways that diabetics can **control** their blood sugar levels.

1. ....

2. ....

3. ....

Q5 A lot of **research** is being done by scientists into the **treatment** of diabetes.

a) **i)** Describe a major improvement that has been made to the **source** of the insulin used by diabetics.

....

....

ii) What is the main advantage of using this new source of insulin?

....

b) **i)** What **surgical** treatment can be used to cure type 1 diabetes?

....

ii) Describe **two problems** with the treatment you have named.

....

....

c) Scientists are constantly researching new treatments and cures for diabetes.
Name **two** treatments that are currently in development.

1. ....

2. ....

Top Tips: Although diabetes is a serious disease, many diabetics are able to control their blood sugar levels and carry on with normal lives. Sir Steve Redgrave even won a gold medal at the Olympics after he had been diagnosed with type 1 diabetes.

Mixed Questions — Biology 3a

Q1 We each have around 600 million **alveoli** in our lungs. This ensures that we can get enough oxygen into our bloodstream and remove the waste carbon dioxide from it.

a) Describe **four** ways in which the alveoli are specialised to maximise gas exchange.

alveolis have a larger surface area to maximise gas exchange. It has moist linings, a good flow of blood supply and finally very thin walls.

b) i) Which **cells** in the blood carry the oxygen that has diffused through the alveoli walls?

red blood cells

ii) Which **substance** in the cell combines with the oxygen? haemoglobic.

iii) How are the cells **adapted** to carry oxygen?

they have no nucleus, are biconcave shaped, large surface area.

Q2 The diagram shows a **specialised cell**.

a) Name the cell shown.

root hair cell.

b) Explain how the cell's **shape** helps it to absorb **water**.

It has hairs that are long which absorbs water which means it has a large surface area.

c) The cell is exposed to a poison that stops respiration. Why would this affect the uptake of **minerals** but not the uptake of **water**?

d) i) Water absorbed by the roots is lost through the leaves as vapour. What process does it escape by?

~~diffusion~~ transpiration

ii) Under what conditions is water loss at its greatest?

iii) Name another gas that escapes out of a leaf. Oxygen.

Human Impact on the Environment

Q1 Circle the correct word to complete each sentence below.

a) The size of the human population now is **bigger** / **smaller** than it was 1000 years ago.

b) The growth of the human population now is **slower** / **faster** than it was 1000 years ago.

c) The human impact on the environment now is **less** / **greater** than it was 1000 years ago.

Q2 One way to assess a person's impact on the Earth is to use an **ecological footprint**. This involves calculating **how many Earths** would be needed if everyone lived like that person. It takes into account things like the amount of **waste** the person produces and how much **energy** they use.

a) Two men calculate their ecological footprints. Eight Earths would be needed to support everyone in the way John lives. Half an Earth would be enough to support everyone in the way Derek lives.

i) One of the men lives in a UK city, and one in rural Kenya. Who is more likely to live where?

....

ii) Tick any of the following that are possible reasons for the difference in results.

- [ ] John buys more belongings, which use more raw materials to manufacture.
- [ ] John has central heating in his home but Derek has a wood fire.
- [ ] John throws away less waste.
- [ ] John drives a car and Derek rides a bicycle.

b) Suggest one thing John could do to reduce the size of his ecological footprint.

....

Q3 Some water voles have been nesting in an area of marsh land.
A farmer wants to **drain** half of the marsh to grow crops.

a) i) State whether you would expect the population of voles to increase or decrease.

....

ii) Give **one** reason for your answer to part **i**).

....

....

b) Name **two** human activities, apart from farming, that reduce the amount of land available for animals and plants.

1. ....

2. ....

Human Impact on the Environment

Q4 The size of the Earth's **population** has an impact on our **environment**.

a) Use the table below to plot a graph on the grid, showing how the world's human population has changed over the last 1000 years.

NO. OF PEOPLE (BILLIONS)	YEAR
0.3	1000
0.4	1200
0.4	1400
0.6	1600
1.0	1800
1.7	1900
6.1	2000

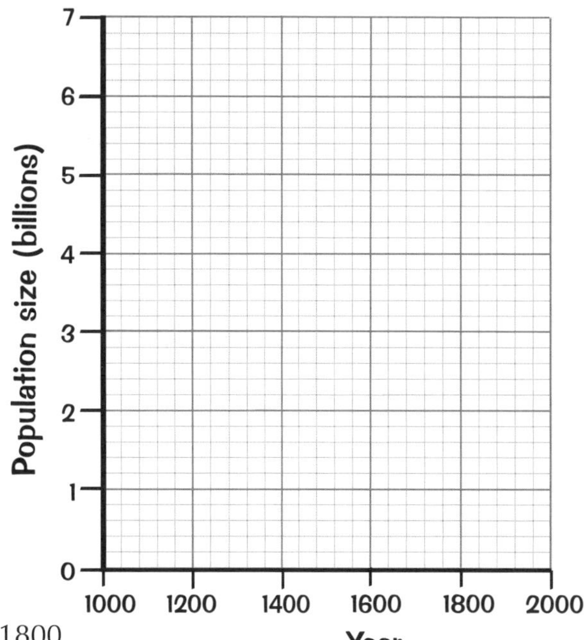

b) Suggest two reasons for the sudden increase after 1800.

....

....

c) What effect is an increasing population having on the amount of waste we produce?

....

Q5 As the human population **grows** we need more **food**. Modern farming methods can increase the amount of food grown, but they may harm the environment.

a) Give three types of chemicals used in modern farming.

1. ....

2. ....

3. ....

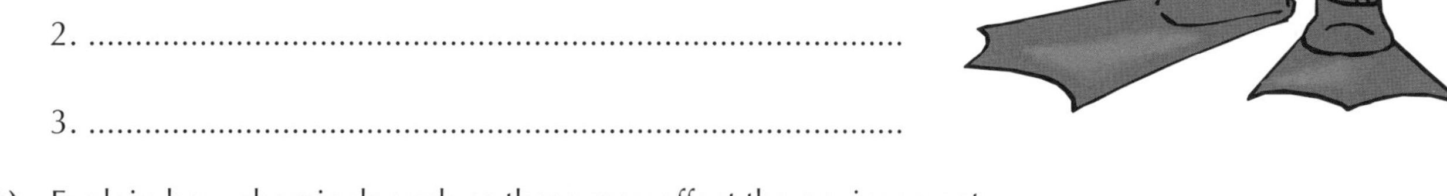

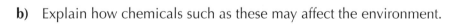

b) Explain how chemicals such as these may affect the environment.

....

....

....

Top Tips: There's lots to think about with this topic. It's the kind of thing you might get a longer answer question on in an exam, where you have to weigh up all the different arguments. And examiners can't get enough of that graph where the human population goes shooting up — they love it.

Carbon Dioxide and the Greenhouse Effect

Q1 Complete the following passage using some of the words from the list below.

more sequestered oceans less burning
global warming carbon dioxide making

Carbon is present in the atmosphere as .... (CO_2). Lots of processes lead to CO_2 being released, for example by .... fossil fuels. Too much CO_2 in the atmosphere causes ....

However, CO_2 can be .... ('locked up') in natural stores, including ...., lakes and ponds. Storing CO_2 in these ways is really important because it means there is .... CO_2 in the atmosphere.

Q2 Underline the statements below about the greenhouse effect that are **true**.

The greenhouse effect is needed for life on Earth as we know it.

Greenhouse gases include carbon dioxide and sulfur dioxide.

The greenhouse effect causes acid rain.

Increasing amounts of greenhouse gases is causing global warming.

Q3 The Earth receives energy from the **Sun**. It radiates much of this energy back towards space.

a) Explain the role of the greenhouse gases in keeping the Earth warm.

....

....

....

b) What would happen if there were no greenhouse gases?

....

....

c) In recent years the amounts of greenhouse gases in the atmosphere have increased.
Explain how this leads to global warming.

....

....

Deforestation and the Destruction of Peat Bogs

Q1 **Deforestation** means **cutting down** forests. It can lead to big environmental problems.

a) Explain how deforestation leads to an increase in the amount of carbon dioxide in the atmosphere.

....

....

....

....

b) Some forest is cleared to provide land for farming.
Tick the boxes to show whether these statements are true or false.

	True	False
i) Rearing cattle decreases the amount of methane released into the atmosphere.	☐	☐
ii) Rice is grown in warm, waterlogged conditions that are ideal for decomposers. Decomposers produce methane.	☐	☐

c) Give **two** reasons, apart from creating more farmland, why humans cut forests down.

....

....

Q2 **Ecosystems** like rainforests contain many different **species**. If we destroy rainforests we risk making species extinct and **reducing biodiversity**.

a) Define the term '**biodiversity**'.

....

b) Describe **one** implication for humans of reducing biodiversity.

....

Q3 The destruction of **peat bogs** releases **carbon dioxide** into the atmosphere.

a) Briefly describe how peat is formed.

....

....

b) Explain why draining a peat bog increases the level of carbon dioxide in the atmosphere.

....

....

c) Suggest **one** thing that a **gardener** could do to help reduce the number of peat bogs being drained.

....

Climate Change

Q1 These statements help explain how **global warming** may lead to floods. Use them to complete the **flow chart** below, which has one box filled in to start you off.

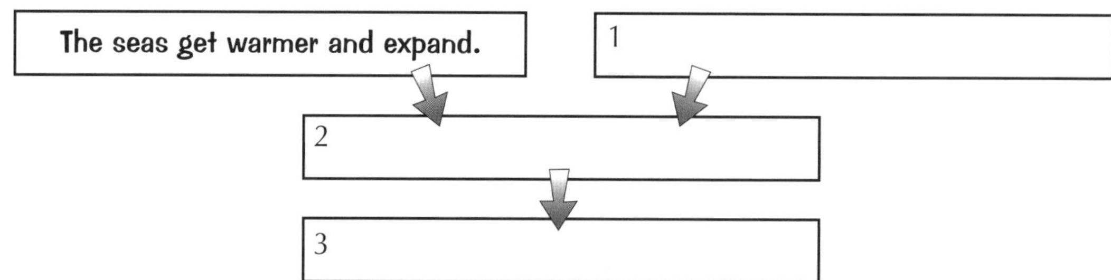
Low-lying areas are at risk of flooding.
Higher temperatures make ice melt.
Sea levels start to rise.
The seas get warmer and expand.
1
2
3

Q2 Circle the correct words to complete the sentences about **global warming** below.

a) Global warming could **increase** / **reduce** biodiversity.

b) As northern areas get warmer, some birds might migrate further **north** / **south**.

c) Species that need **warmer** / **cooler** temperatures to survive may become **more** / **less** widely distributed as the conditions they thrive in exist over a smaller area.

d) Global warming may change weather patterns across the world, leading to more **mild** / **extreme** weather in many places.

Q3 Two university students carried out **observations**. Student A noticed that a glacier was melting. Student B noticed that daffodils were flowering earlier in 2006 than in 2005. Both students concluded that this was due to **global warming**. Are they right? Explain your answer.

....

....

Q4 There's a **scientific consensus** that global warming is happening. This means scientists have collected enough **evidence** to accept the **hypothesis**.

a) What is meant by evidence and hypothesis?

evidence: ....

hypothesis: ....

b) Give examples of the sort of data that scientists are collecting about climate change.

....

....

Biofuels

Q1 In the sentences below, circle the correct word.

a) Fermentation is a form of **digestion** / **respiration**.

b) Fermentation is **aerobic** / **anaerobic**.

c) Fermentation by yeast produces **ethanol** / **methane**.

d) **Ethanol** / **Biogas** can be mixed with petrol and used to fuel cars — this is known as gasohol.

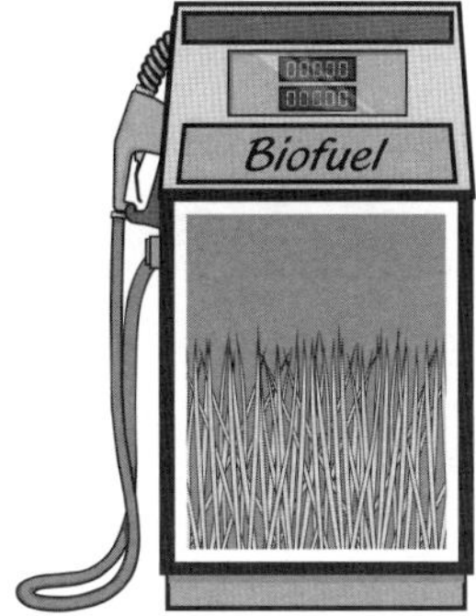

Q2 **Ethanol** is a biofuel that can be made from specially grown crops. Fill in the gaps in the sentences below about ethanol.

a) Ethanol is made by fermenting sugar, such as ....

b) The sugar is extracted from crops, such as ....

Q3 Use the words below to fill in the gaps and complete the passage about **biogas**.

batch	generator	fermented	heating	turbine	waste	carbohydrates

Biogas can be made in a container called a ...., either by continuous production or by .... production. It is made from plant and animal .... which contains .... and is .... by microorganisms.

Biogas could be used for ...., or even to power a .... for making electricity.

Q4 Below are some fairly straightforward questions about **biogas**. Great.

a) Name the main components of biogas.

....

b) Name **two** materials that might be used as food for the microorganisms used in producing biogas.

....

....

Using Biogas Generators

Q1 Kapilisha did an experiment to produce **biogas** in the laboratory. After setting up the experiment, she left the apparatus in a warm place for five weeks. The diagram below shows her apparatus.

a) Describe the process going on inside the plastic bottle.

....

....

....

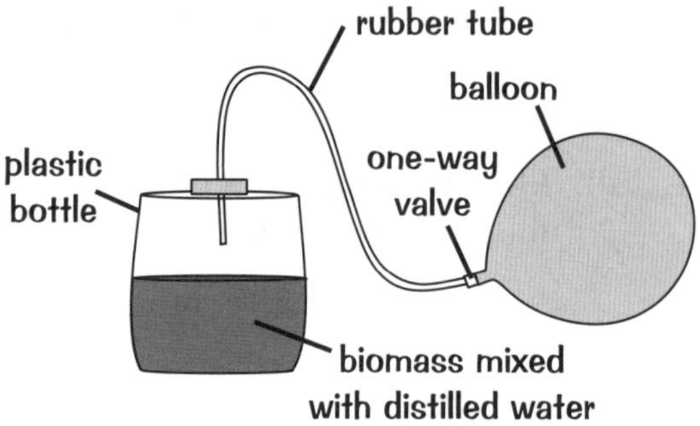

b) If biogas was produced, what change would be visible after a few weeks?

....

c) Explain why the bottle was left in a **warm** place during the five weeks.

....

....

Q2 Professor Wiggins did an experiment to find the best **temperature** for **biogas production**. The graph below shows what she found.

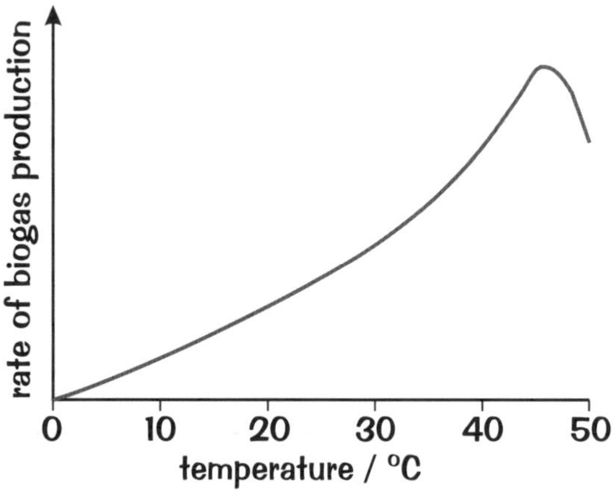

a) What is the best temperature for biogas production? ....

b) Professor Wiggins decided to set up her biogas generator at a temperature **slightly below** the best temperature. Suggest a reason for this.

....

....

....

c) Suggest **two** variables apart from temperature that might also affect the rate of biogas production.

....

....

d) Sewage can be used for biogas production, but it is important that the sewage contains as few chemical toxins as possible. Explain why this is important.

....

....

Using Biogas Generators

Q3 Biogas may be produced in a **batch** or **continuous** generator from waste materials, e.g. animal waste. Circle the correct words below to describe how a batch and continuous generator differ.

a) In a **batch** / **continuous** generator, waste is usually loaded manually.

b) A **batch** / **continuous** generator is the best choice for large-scale production.

c) In a continuous generator, waste is added **at intervals** / **all the time**.

d) In a **batch** / **continuous** generator, biogas is produced at a steady rate.

Q4 In a village in South America, a **biogas generator** was built.

a) Suggest reasons for the following features of the design:

i) The generator was built some distance away from houses in the village.

....

ii) The generator was built close to fields where animals were grazing.

....

iii) The generator was covered with insulating material.

....

b) Describe **two** possible advantages for the villagers in having a biogas generator like this.

....

....

Q5 The diagram on the right shows a **biogas generator system**.

a) The energy in biogas originally came from the **Sun**. Explain how.

....

....

....

b) Biogas is sometimes described as being '**carbon neutral**'.

i) Explain why biogas is carbon neutral.

....

....

ii) Name **two other** reasons why biogas is less damaging to the environment than many fuels.

....

....

Managing Food Production

Q1 Three different **food chains** are shown here.

Grass → Cattle → Human

Pondweed → Small fish → Salmon → Human

Wheat → Human

a) Circle the food chain that shows the most **efficient** production of **food** for **humans**.

b) Explain your choice.

....

Q2 **Mycoprotein** is used to make protein-rich **meat substitutes** for vegetarian meals.

a) Name the fungus that is used to produce mycoprotein.

....

b) Complete this passage about making mycoprotein using some of the words from the list below.

oxygen, purified, vegetable oil, fermenters, recycled, carbon dioxide, glucose syrup

The fungus is grown in ...., using .... as food. The fungus respires aerobically, so .... is supplied, together with nitrogen and other minerals. When enough mycoprotein has grown, it is harvested and then ....

Q3 In the UK a lot of our pork comes from **intensively farmed** pigs.

a) Explain what is meant by 'intensive farming'.

....

....

b) Explain why intensively farming pigs makes pork production more efficient.

....

....

....

c) Give one benefit to the consumer of farming pigs intensively.

....

Top Tips: Energy and biomass are lost every time you move up a stage in a food chain. So reducing the number of stages in a food chain increases the efficiency of food production.

Problems With Food Production and Distribution

Q1 The structure of the UK **egg industry** has changed in recent years. The table below shows the percentages of the egg market represented by three methods of chicken farming — **laying** (battery hens), **barn** (hens that roam freely indoors) and **free range** (hens that roam freely outdoors).

	Percentage of egg market for each type of chicken farming		
Year	Laying	Barn	Free range
1999	78	6	16
2001	72	5	23
2003	69	6	25
2005	66	7	27
Change			

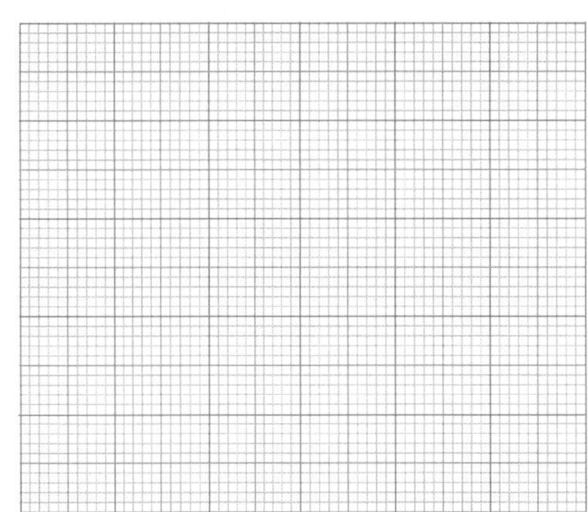

a) Use this data to make a bar chart on the grid above.

b) Calculate the change in the percentage of the market held by each farming type between 1999 and 2005. Write your answers in the spaces on the table.

final % – initial %

c) Suggest a reason for the changes.

....

....

Q2 Explain why products that have lots of '**food miles**' can be bad for the **environment**.

....

....

....

Q3 **Overfishing** has caused a large fall in the number of fish in our oceans.

a) Explain how **fishing quotas** can help to maintain fish stocks.

....

....

b) Continuing to fish, whilst maintaining fish stocks at a level where the fish can still breed, is an example of **sustainable food production**.
What is meant by 'sustainable food production'?

....

....

Mixed Questions — Biology 3b

Q1 **Intensive farming** is one way of making food production more **efficient**.

a) Circle the correct words to complete the sentences below about the problems of intensive farming.

i) The **warm** / **crowded** conditions make it **easy** / **hard** for diseases to spread.

ii) The animals are frequently given **pesticides** / **antibiotics**, which get into the human food chain.

iii) Heating the animal buildings **increases** / **decreases** a farm's energy use.

b) Martin intensively farms turkeys. He wants to use the turkeys' waste to produce energy. Name a fuel that Martin could make using the animal waste.

....

Q2 The graph below shows changes in **global temperature** since 1859.

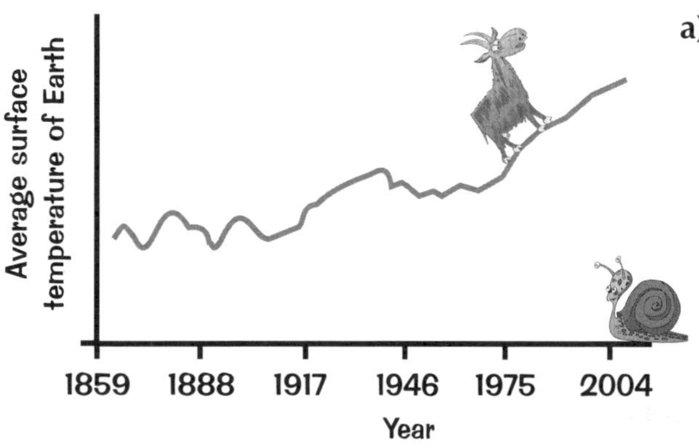

a) Describe the trend shown on the graph.

....

....

....

b) The next graph shows how current levels of three gases compare to their levels before the Industrial Revolution.

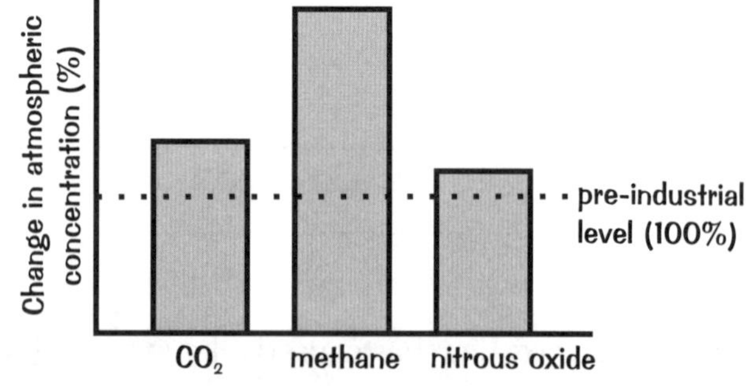

i) Which gas has had the biggest percentage increase in concentration?

....

ii) Give one source of this gas.

....

c) What conclusion can you draw from these two graphs? Did one of the changes definitely cause the other?

....

....

....

History of the Periodic Table

Q1 Complete the sentences below.

a) In the modern periodic table, the elements are ordered by their Their relative atomic mass

b) Before this, the known elements were arranged in order by their Their physical and chemical propoties

Q2 Tick the boxes to show whether the following statements about **Mendeleev's** Table of Elements are **true** or **false**.

	True	False
a) Mendeleev left gaps in the table that were later filled.	✓	
b) Mendeleev arranged the elements in order of increasing atomic number.	✓	
c) Mendeleev was able to predict the properties of undiscovered elements.	✓	✗
d) Elements with similar properties appeared in the same rows.	✗	✓

Q3 Mendeleev left **gaps** in his Table of Elements to keep elements with similar properties in the same groups. He predicted that elements would eventually be discovered to fill the gaps. For example, he predicted the discovery of an element that would fill a gap in his Group 4 and called it '**ekasilicon**'.

The table shows the **densities** of known elements in this group.

Element	Density g/cm³
carbon	2.27
silicon	2.33
'ekasilicon'	
tin	7.29
lead	11.34

a) 'Ekasilicon' was eventually discovered and given another name.
Use the information in the table to decide which of the elements below is 'ekasilicon'.
Circle your choice.

palladium, 12.02 g/cm³ **germanium, 5.32 g/cm³** **beryllium, 1.85 g/cm³** **copper, 8.93 g/cm³**

b) i) Before Mendeleev, **Newlands** had already tried to classify the known elements.
Give **one** similarity between Mendeleev's arrangement and Newlands' earlier attempt.

Arranged them in the same vertical groups.

ii) What was the main **difference** between their approaches?

Mendleev left spaces.

iii) Give **one problem** with Newlands' attempt.

He mixed up the metals with non metals

Q4 Explain where the modern **periodic table** gets its name from.

Because there was a periodic pattern that was noticed in the properties of the elements

The Modern Periodic Table

Q1 Use the words below to complete the passage about the periodic table.

properties	fun	chemical	atomic number	predicting	discovered

At first scientists just treated the periodic table as a bit of ..fun.................................. .
However, scientists started to realise that the periodic table could be a useful tool for ..predicting...................... the ..propeties...................... of elements. Once electrons, protons and neutrons were .....discovered................, the periodic table was arranged in order of ..atomic number....... . The electronic structure of elements can then be used to predict their ..chemical.................. properties.

Q2 The **electron arrangements** of some atoms are shown below.

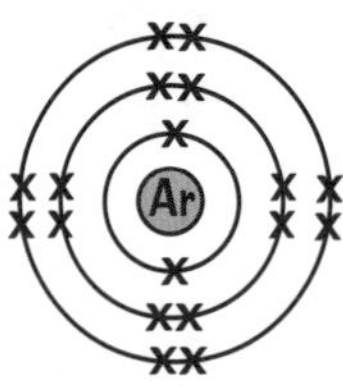

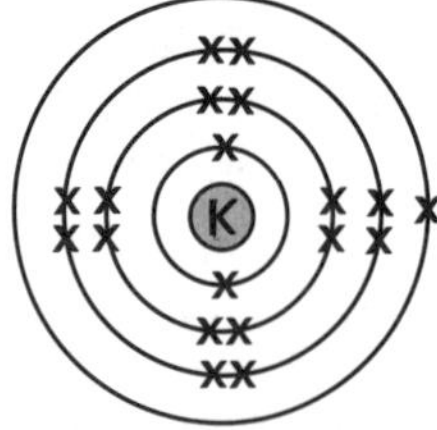

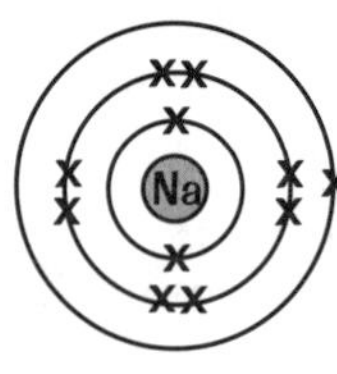

a) In which of these atoms is the outermost electron **furthest** from the nucleus? ..K....................

b) In which of these atoms is the outermost electron **least shielded** from the nucleus? ..Li.........

c) In which of these atoms is the outermost electron **most easily lost**? ..~~Ar~~.......~~Na~~.. K

Q3 A periodic table is shown with **electronic structures** for some of the elements.

1	2		3	4	5	6	7	0
		H 1						He 2
Li 2,1	Be 2,2		B 2,3	C 2,4	N 2,5	O	F 2,7	Ne 2,8
Na 2,8,1	Mg		Al 2,8,3	Si 2,8,4	P 2,8,5	S	Cl 2,8,7	Ar 2,8,8
K 2,8,8,1	Ca 2,8,8,2	Transition metals						

a) How does the number of electrons in the outer shell of each atom relate to the **group** it is in?

The amount of electrons on the outer cell are the same as the group.

b) Write down the electronic structures for:

magnesium ..2,8,2.................. oxygen ~~2,8,6~~ 2,6........... sulfur ..2,8,~~7~~ 6............

c) Is fluorine likely to be more or less reactive than chlorine? Explain your answer.

less because the elements get more reactive as the go down the colum, more because flourine is on top of the halegons

The Modern Periodic Table

Q4 The table shows the electronic structure for some **Group 1** and **Group 7** elements.

It's an element, my dear Watson

Group 1	Electronic Structure	Group 7	Electronic Structure
Li	2, 1	F	2, 7
Na	2, 8, 1	Cl	2, 8, 7
K	2, 8, 8, 1	Br	2, 8, 18, 7

Bromine's got more than 8 electrons in one of its shells — don't worry about that for now. The important thing is the number of electrons in its outer shell.

a) i) Why do potassium atoms lose their outer electron more easily than lithium atoms?

Because lithium only has two shells which means that its harder too lose its outer electron

ii) Does this make potassium more or less reactive than lithium? more

b) i) Explain why fluorine atoms attract electrons more strongly than bromine atoms.

Because it needs one electron to complete its outershell

ii) Explain the trend in the reactivities of the Group 7 elements in terms of nuclear attraction.

The more they go down the column it makes the nuclear attraction greater to get a full outshell

Q5 The electron arrangement for **potassium** is shown to the right.

a) In which group of the periodic table would you expect to find potassium?

1

b) There are two elements in the same group as potassium that have smaller atomic numbers. Explain whether you would expect these elements to be more or less reactive than potassium.

less reactive Because there are more shells which takes it further away from the nucleas making it hard for the nucleus to attract more

Group 1 — The Alkali Metals

Q1 Indicate whether the statements below about the alkali metals are **true** or **false**.

		True	False
a)	They are keen to gain electrons to form 1^+ ions.		
b)	They always form covalent compounds.		
c)	They have to be stored in oil.		
d)	Their atoms all have a single electron in the outer shell.		
e)	They form solid white compounds that dissolve in water to form white solutions.		

Q2 Circle the correct word(s) from each pair to complete the passage below.

Sodium reacts vigorously with water producing **sodium dioxide** / **sodium hydroxide** and **hydrogen** / **oxygen** gas. When it reacts, it loses its outer **proton** / **electron**, forming an ionic compound where the sodium ion has a **positive** / **negative** charge.

Q3 The table shows the **reactivity** of some Group 1 metals.

Element
Li
Na
K
Rb
Cs

reactivity increases

Explain the pattern of reactivity shown in the table.

Q4 Archibald put a piece of **lithium** into a beaker of water.

a) Explain why the lithium floated on top of the water.

b) After the reaction had finished, Archibald tested the water with universal indicator. Would the solution be acidic, alkaline or neutral? Circle the correct word.

acidic **alkaline** **neutral**

c) i) Write a **word equation** for the reaction.

ii) Write a **balanced symbol equation** for the reaction. Include the state symbols.

Top Tips: It's all about keeping up with the trends. Make sure you know what happens to the properties and reactions of the alkali metals as you go down the periodic table.

Group 7 — The Halogens

Q1 Say whether these statements are **true** or **false**.

		True	False
a)	Chlorine gas is made up of molecules which each contain three chlorine atoms.		✓
b)	The further down the group a halogen is, the harder it is for it to gain an electron.	✓	
c)	Halide ions have a charge of 1^+.		✓
d)	The melting points of the halogens increase down the group.	✓	

Q2 Draw lines to match the phrases and complete the sentences.

The halogens exist as molecules ...	... to form ionic compounds.
A more reactive halogen ...	... decreases as you move down the group.
The halogens react with metals ...	... which are pairs of atoms.
The reactivity of the halogens ...	... will displace a less reactive one.

Q3 **Iron** can be reacted with **bromine**.
An **orange solid** forms on the sides of the test tube.

bromine
iron wool
HEAT

a) Name the compound formed. Iron bromide

b) What type of bonding is present in this compound?

ionic

Q4 Equal volumes of **bromine water** were added to two test tubes, each containing a different **potassium halide solution**. The results are shown in the table.

SOLUTION	RESULT
potassium chloride	no change
potassium iodide	solution changed colour

a) Explain these results.

Because Bromine ~~sol~~ replaces the ones only beneath it, this means Chloride wouldn't be replaced. But iodide is beneath bromine which means it is replaceable

b) Write a **balanced symbol equation** (including state symbols) for the reaction in the iodide solution.

$Br_{2(aq)}$ + 2KI (aq) → 2KBr (aq) + I_2 (aq)

Transition Elements

Q1 Transition elements are **metals**.

Shade the area where **transition metals** are found on this periodic table:

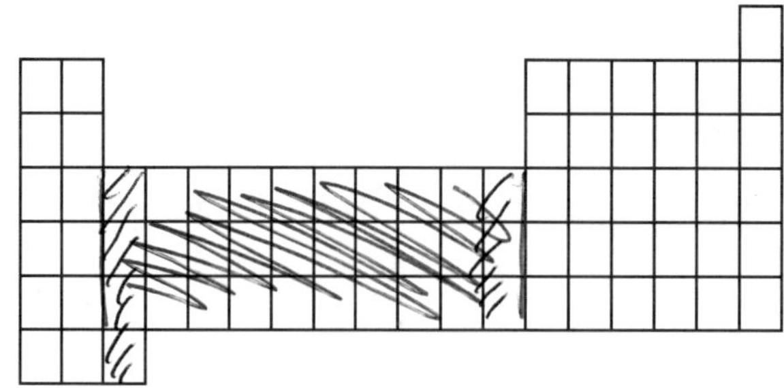

Q2 Complete the passage below by circling the correct word(s) from each pair.

The transition metals react **more / less** vigorously with oxygen and water than Group 1 metals. They have **higher / lower** densities and most have **lower / higher** melting points than Group 1 metals. They are also **harder / softer** than Group 1 metals. Their compounds are **coloured / shiny**. These compounds and the metals themselves, are effective **fuels / catalysts** in many reactions.

Q3 Which one of the following properties applies to **all** transition metals? Circle your answers.

high density   high melting point   poor conductivity

Q4 Transition metals and their compounds often make good catalysts.

a) Draw lines to match the metals and compounds below to the reactions they catalyse.

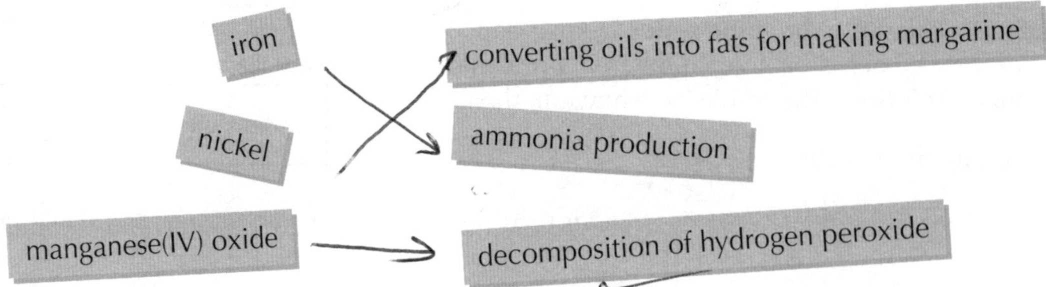

b) Transition metals often form more than one ion.
Write down two different ions formed by:

i) Iron ....

ii) Copper ....

iii) Chromium ....

Transition Elements

Q5 'Chemical gardens' can be made by sprinkling **transition metal salts** into **sodium silicate solution**. Transition metal silicate crystals grow upwards as shown.

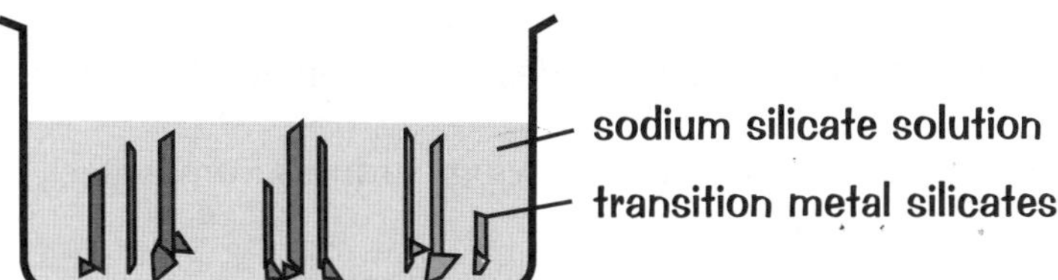

a) Satoru decides to make a chemical garden. He sprinkles **iron(II) sulfate**, **iron(III) chloride** and **copper sulfate** crystals into sodium silicate solution. What would he see? Circle your answer.

crystals of different colours   colourless crystals

b) Satoru decides to make another chemical garden. This time he adds **calcium chloride** crystals to the sodium silicate solution. How would the crystals in this chemical garden be **different** from the ones in his first chemical garden? Explain your answer.

Because he will have transition metal chlorides not transition metal silicates which means they would be different colours.

Q6 Read the description of **metal X** and answer the question that follows.

'Metal X is found in the block of elements between groups 2 and 3 in the periodic table. It has a melting point of 1860 °C and a density of 7.2 g/cm³. The metal is used to provide the attractive shiny coating on motorbikes and bathroom taps. The metal forms two coloured chlorides, XCl_2 (blue) and XCl_3 (green).'

Identify six pieces of evidence in the passage which suggest that metal X is a transition metal.

1. Metal x is found in the block between group 2 and 3
2. Its melting point of 1860°c
3. Density 7.2g
4. They have an attractive shiny coating
5. The metal forms coloured chlorides
6. XCl_2 (blue) XCl_3 (green) - ionic bond with chloride - have 2 different oxidation states.

Top Tips: Transition elements do have the properties you would expect a bog standard metal to have. But that's not enough for them so they have some fancy properties of their own. Posers.

Hardness of Water

Q1 State whether the sentences below are true or false.

a) Water which passes over rocks can become hard. True

b) Water can be softened by removing chloride and carbonate ions from the water. True

c) Adding sodium chloride is one way of removing hardness from water. False

d) Scale is formed when soap is used with hard water. True

e) You can remove the hardness from water by adding sodium carbonate. ~~True~~ false

f) Water hardness is caused by Ca^{2+} and Mg^{2+} ions. true

g) Soapless detergents do not form scum. ~~False~~ true

h) Less soap is needed to form a lather with hard water. False

Q2 Hard water can cause the build-up of **scale** in pipes, boilers and kettles.

a) Why can this be a problem with kettles?

Because it forms a barrier around the pipes and is more time to heat

b) Give two **benefits** of hard water.

1. To provide calcium for teeth and bones

2. Good for your health reducing heart diseases

Q3 There are two types of **hardness**.

Draw lines to match the type of hardness to its cause.

Permanent	Hydrogencarbonate ions
Temporary	Dissolved calcium sulfate

Q4 An **ion exchange column** can be used to remove the hardness from water.

a) Explain how hard water becomes soft when it is passed through an **ion exchange column**.

Because it removes the calcium and magnesium and replaces it sodium

b) Does this method work for permanent hardness, temporary hardness, or both?

Permenant hardness

Hardness of Water

Q5 In an experiment to compare the **hardness** of three different water sources, soap solution was added to samples using a burette. Five drops were added at a time until a lasting lather was formed. Fresh samples of the water were boiled and the experiment was repeated.

a) When the samples of hard water were boiled in a beaker, a white precipitate formed.

$$Ca(HCO_3)_{2(aq)} \rightarrow CaCO_{3(s)} + H_2O_{(l)} + CO_{2(g)}$$

Give the chemical name of the white precipitate formed.

....

b) The results for the experiment are shown in the table below.

Source	Drops of soap solution needed to produce a lather using unboiled sample	Drops of soap solution needed to produce a lather using boiled sample
A	35	5
B	30	15
C	5	5

Write the correct letters in the gaps below to complete the sentences about the results.

i) Source .... and .... are hard water.

ii) Source .... contains both temporary and permanent hardness.

iii) Source .... contains only temporary hardness.

iv) Source .... is soft water.

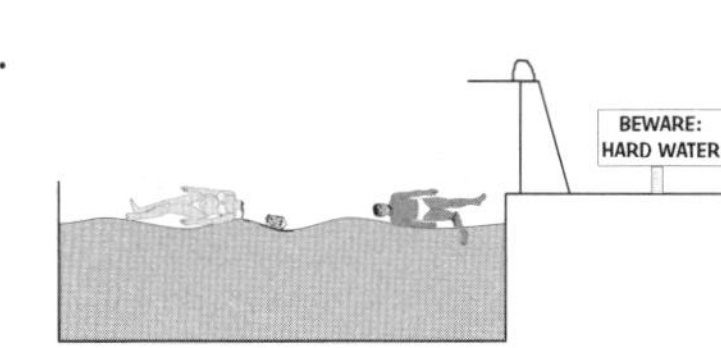

c) **i)** Explain how you can tell which source contains permanent hardness.

....

ii) Give the name of a chemical that can be added to permanent hard water to soften it.

....

d) **i)** Suggest which source contains the most temporary hardness. ....

ii) Explain your answer.

....

....

Top Tips: Hard water isn't very exciting, but at least it's not, well, hard. Make sure you know how to soften up the two different types of hardness. Remember that there's more than one tactic.

Water Quality

Q1 Drinking water needs to be good quality.

a) Which type of water is most pure? Circle your answer.

tap water **river water** **distilled water** **sea water**

b) Explain why this type of water is not generally used as drinking water.

....

Q2 Water from reservoirs is treated in a **water treatment works**.

The diagram below shows the stages of a water treatment process.

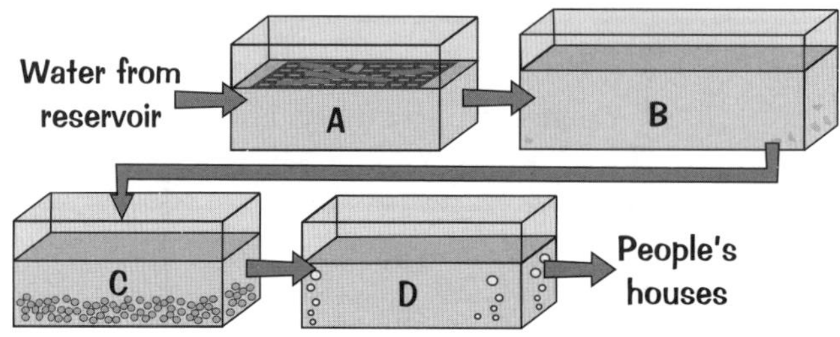

Match stages A-D to the explanations below by writing the correct letters in the boxes.

☐ Chlorine is added to kill any remaining harmful microbes.

☐ Chemicals are added to make solids and microbes stick together and fall to the bottom.

☐ The water passes through a mesh screen to remove bits like twigs.

☐ The water is filtered to remove all solids.

Q3 **Chlorine** and **fluoride** can be added to drinking water.

a) Use the words below to fill the gaps in the passage.

harmless	toxic	cancer	bone	tooth decay	disease	heart disease

Fluoride is sometimes added to drinking water because it helps reduce .... Chlorine is added to water to prevent .... However, high doses of fluoride have been linked to .... and .... problems. Chlorine can react with natural substances in water to produce .... by-products.

b) Explain how people can remove the chlorine taste from the water they drink.

....

Reversible Reactions

Q1 Use words from the list below to complete the following sentences about **reversible reactions**.

escape	reactants	catalysts	closed	products	react	balance

In a reversible reaction, the ....products.... of the reaction can themselves ....react.... to give the original ....reactants.... .

At equilibrium, the amounts of reactants and products reach a ....balance.... .

To reach equilibrium the reaction must happen in a ....closed.... system, where products and reactants can't ....escape.... .

Q2 Look at this diagram of a **reversible reaction**.

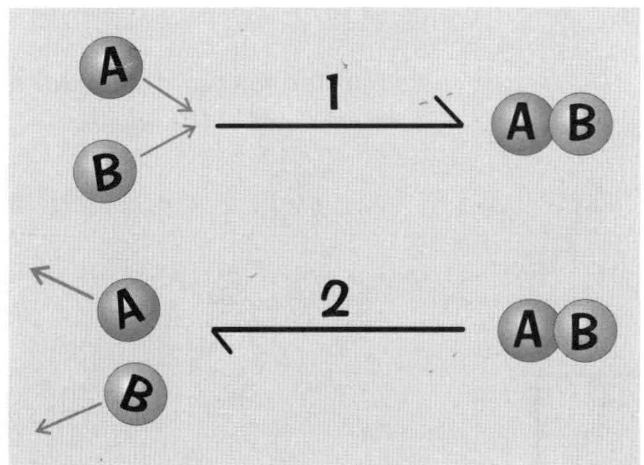

The reaction going from left to right is called the forward reaction.

a) For the forward reaction:

i) give the reactant(s) ....A + B....

ii) give the product(s) ....AB....

b) i) Here are two labels:

X product splits up
Y reactants combine

Which of these labels goes in position 1 — X or Y? ....Y....

ii) Which label goes in position 2 — X or Y? ....X....

c) Write the equation for the reversible reaction. ....$A + B \rightleftharpoons AB$....

d) Complete the sentence by circling the correct phrase.

At equilibrium, the forward and backward reactions happen **at different rates / at zero rate / at the same rate.**

Q3 Which of these statements about reversible reactions are **true** and which are **false**?

		True	False
a)	The position of equilibrium depends on the reaction conditions.	✓	
b)	Upon reaching equilibrium, the reactions stop taking place.		✓
c)	You can move the position of equilibrium to get more product.	✓	
d)	At equilibrium there will always be equal quantities of products and reactants.		✓

Reversible Reactions

Q4 Substances A and B react to produce substances C and D in a reversible reaction.

$$2A_{(g)} + B_{(g)} \rightleftharpoons 2C_{(g)} + D_{(g)}$$

a) The forward reaction is **exothermic**.
Does the backward reaction give out or take in heat?
Explain your answer.

No, its endothermic so it takes in heat because

b) If the **temperature** is raised, which reaction will increase, the forward or the backward reaction?

~~Foward~~ backwards

c) Explain why changing the temperature of a reversible reaction always affect the position of equilibrium.

Because the endothermic reaction will be increased by a higher temperature

d) What effect will changing the **pressure** have on the position of equilibrium of this reaction? Explain your answer.

Look at the number of molecules on each side of the reaction.

It won't change sinc theres equal moles of gas on both sides.

Q5 a) In this reaction: $2SO_{2(g)} + O_{2(g)} \rightleftharpoons 2SO_{3(g)}$

i) Which reaction, forward or backward, is accompanied by a **decrease** in volume?
Explain your answer.

Its forward since its changing from 3 moles of gas to 2 moles of gas.

ii) How will increasing the pressure affect the position of equilibrium in this reaction?

It would increase the forward reaction

b) What does adding a catalyst to a reversible reaction do? Circle the correct letter.

A It moves the equilibrium position towards the products.

B It makes the reaction achieve equilibrium more quickly.

C It moves the equilibrium position towards the reactants.

D It causes a decrease in pressure.

c) What happens to the amount of product when you use a catalyst? The amount of product will stay the same.

The Haber Process

Q1 The Haber process is used to make **ammonia** which is used to produce fertilisers.

a) Complete the equation for the reaction below.

$$N_{2(g)} + 3H_{2(g)} \rightleftharpoons 2NH_{3(g)}$$

b) Give one source of each of the two reactants in the forward reaction.

N2 is from the air and 3H2 is from natural gases

Q2 The **industrial conditions** for the Haber process are carefully chosen.

a) What conditions are used? Tick one box.

☐ 1000 atmospheres, 450 °C	☐ 200 atmospheres, 1000 °C	☐ 450 atmospheres, 200 °C	☑ 200 atmospheres, 450 °C

b) Give two reasons why the pressure used is chosen.

1. It is high enough to increase the foward reaction.
2. It isn't too expensive.

Q3 In the Haber process reaction, the forward reaction is **exothermic**.

a) What effect will raising the temperature have on the **amount** of ammonia formed?

It would decrease since 2NH3 is endothermic

b) Explain why a high temperature is used industrially.

Speeds the collusion and strength of collusion.

c) What happens to the leftover nitrogen and hydrogen? It is recycled then reused.

Q4 The Haber process uses an **iron catalyst**.

a) What effect does this have on the % yield? no effect

b) Iron catalysts are relatively cheap. What effect does using one have on the **cost** of producing the ammonia? Explain your answer.

It would decrease the cost of producing ammonia since it uses lower pressure.

Top Tips: Changing the conditions in a reversible reaction to get more product sounds great, but don't forget that these conditions might be too difficult or expensive for factories to produce, or they might mean a reaction that's too slow to be profitable.

Alcohols

Q1 **Alcohols** are a common group of chemicals.

Complete the following table.

Alcohol	No. of Carbon Atoms	Molecular Formula	Displayed Formula
Methanol			
	2		
Propanol		C_3H_7OH	

Q2 The molecular formula for **propanol** can be written as $\mathbf{C_3H_7OH}$ or as $\mathbf{C_3H_8O}$.

a) What is the functional group found in all alcohols? ....

b) Explain why it is better to write ethanol's formula as C_3H_7OH.

....

Q3 Alcohols are **flammable**.

a) Give the balanced equation for the reaction that takes place when **ethanol** burns completely in air.

....

b) Choose from the words below to complete the paragraph about ethanol.

fuel diesel non-renewable fermentation lubricant land
more renewable oxidation sunshine petrol less

Ethanol can be mixed with .... and used as a .... for cars. The more ethanol used in the mixture, the .... pollution produced. In some countries ethanol is made by the .... of plants such as sugar cane.

Making ethanol this way uses a natural and .... resource.

The sugar cane can be grown continuously, but you need plenty of .... and ....

Alcohols

Q4 Tick the correct boxes to show whether the following statements are **true** or **false**.

		True	False
a)	Ethanol is the third alcohol in the homologous series.	☐	☐
b)	Ethanol is more toxic than methanol.	☐	☐
c)	Ethanol is the main alcohol used in alcoholic drinks.	☐	☐
d)	Alcohols burn to produce sulphur dioxide and water.	☐	☐
e)	The first three alcohols all dissolve completely in water to form neutral solutions.	☐	☐
f)	Ethanol can damage the liver and brain.	☐	☐
g)	Ethanol reacts with sodium to produce sodium ethoxide and hydrogen.	☐	☐

Q5 **Alcohols** can be used as **solvents**.

Complete the following passage by filling in the gaps using the words provided.

water	oils	dissolve	perfumes	fats	solvents

Alcohols such as methanol and ethanol can .... some compounds that water can, but also substances that water can't — e.g. .... and .... This makes alcohols very useful .... in industry. For example, ethanol is used to make .... It can mix with both the .... (which give the smell) and the .... (that makes up the bulk).

You can use a word more than once if you need to.

Q6 **Meths** (methylated spirits) is ethanol with other substances added to it.

a) One of these substances is a purply-blue dye. Suggest why this is added.

....

b) Give **two** uses of meths.

1. ....

2. ....

Top Tips: Right, listen up. You need to know the **structures**, **formulas**, **properties** and the **reactions** of alcohols. You also need to be able to evaluate all the useful things you can do with them — like using them as a fuel in cars (but I really wouldn't suggest tipping your dad's favourite whisky into his car — he probably won't be best pleased...).

Carboxylic Acids

Q1 Tick the correct boxes to show whether the following statements are **true** or **false**.

		True	False
a)	Carboxylic acids have the functional group –COOH.	☐	☐
b)	There are six carbon atoms in every molecule of propanoic acid.	☐	☐
c)	Ethanoic acid reacts with sodium carbonate to produce sodium ethanoate and water.	☐	☐

Q2 Complete the following table.

Carboxylic acid	No. of Carbon Atoms	Molecular Formula	Displayed Formula
Methanoic Acid			
	2		
		C_2H_5COOH	

Q3 Ethanoic acid can be made by oxidising ethanol.

a) **i)** What can be used to oxidise ethanol? Circle your answer.

a catalyst   microbes   an ester   vinegar

ii) What else can be used to oxidise ethanol?

....

b) When ethanoic acid is dissolved in water it forms a weak acidic solution.

i) Explain why this is.

....

....

ii) Give the common name for a solution of ethanoic acid.

....

c) Hydrochloric acid is a strong acid. Would you expect a solution of hydrochloric acid to have a higher or lower pH than a solution of ethanoic acid with the same concentration?

....

Esters

Q1 Complete the sentences below by circling the correct word from each pair.

a) The fruit flavours used in some sweets are made by mixing man-made **esters** / **alcohols** together.

b) Esters **do** / **don't** mix very well with water, and **do** / **don't** mix well with alcohols.

c) Some esters **are** / **aren't** volatile.

d) Many esters are highly **unreactive** / **flammable**, which can lead to a flash **fire** / **flood**.

e) Esters have the functional group **-COO-** / **-COOH**.

Q2 Look at the **structural formulas** and **chemical names** below.

Circle the ones which refer to **esters**.

H–C(=O)–O–C(H)(H)–C(H)(H)–C(H)(H)–H

propanoic acid

H–C(H)(H)–C(=O)–OH

methyl ethanoate

Q3 **Ethanol** can be reacted with a carboxylic acid to make **ethyl ethanoate**.

a) Name the catalyst used in this reaction.

....

b) Complete the word equation below for this reaction.

ethanol + ... → ethyl ethanoate + ...

Ha ha ha - snort - ha ha ha haaa! You're giving me esterics!

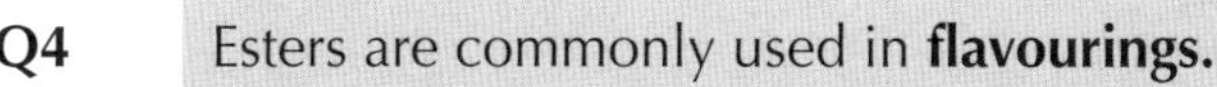

Q4 Esters are commonly used in **flavourings.**

a) Suggest why some people worry about esters being used as **food flavourings**.

....

b) Give **one** other use of esters.

....

Top Tips: Here's a bit of good news. The only ester you need to be able to give the name of in the exam is ethyl ethanoate. Now for the bad news (there's always some). You do need to be able to spot an ester from either its name or structural formula. So, make sure you know what to look for.

Mixed Questions — Chemistry 3a

Q1 A new **perfume**, 'Back2Basics', is being released. The main ingredients are **water**, **alcohol** and a sweet smelling **ester**.

Give **two** properties of esters that make them well suited for use in perfumes.

1. ....

2. ....

Q2 Answer the following questions about the **periodic table**.

a) By what property did Mendeleev arrange the elements in the periodic table?

....

b) What did he do that Newlands didn't?

....

c) If an element is in Group 1, how many electrons will it have in its outer electron shell? ....

d) An ion of an element has a 2^+ charge. Which group is the element most likely to be in? ....

Q3 **Aqueous chlorine**, Cl_2, was added to **potassium bromide solution**, KBr.

a) Complete and **balance** the following chemical equation:

$Cl_{2(aq)}$ + ... $KBr_{(aq)}$ → ....(.......) + ...(.......)

b) Suggest why bromine solution will **not** react with aqueous potassium chloride.

....

Q4 The Haber process is a **reversible reaction**.

a) Write a **balanced symbol equation** for the reaction.

....

b) The Haber process is carried out at a pressure of 200 atmospheres.

i) Does raising the pressure **increase** or **decrease** the rate of the forward reaction? ....

ii) Explain why. ....

....

c) The forward reaction of the Haber process is **exothermic**. If you **increase** the temperature will you increase or decrease the amount of ammonia produced? Circle the correct answer:

increase **decrease**

Mixed Questions — Chemistry 3a

Q5 The table below contains data for three elements, D, E and F, one of which is a **transition metal**.

Element	Melting point (°C)	Electrical conductivity	Density (g/cm^3)
D	98	good	0.97
E	115	poor	2.07
F	1540	good	7.9

a) Which of the elements is likely to be a transition metal? Give two reasons to justify your answer.

....

....

b) Iron is a typical transition metal. Why is it used in the Haber process?

....

Q6 The elements of Group 1, the alkali metals, are reactive metals.

a) Choose an **element** from the list to answer each of these questions. Use the periodic table to help you. Give:

i) an element that is less dense than water. ....

ii) the element with the lowest melting point. ....

iii) the least reactive element. ....

A Rubidium
B Sodium
C Potassium
D Lithium
E Francium
F Caesium

b) Complete the following sentence by circling the correct words.

Alkali metals always form **covalent** / **ionic** compounds. They react with **water** / **air** to produce **hydrogen** / **oxygen** gas and a **hydroxide** / **chloride** solution.

Q7 Hyde added soap solution to samples of water from three different rivers. He recorded the amount of soap needed to create a lasting lather.

Hyde's results are shown in the table on the right.

RIVER	AMOUNT OF SOAP NEEDED (cm^3)	
	PLAIN WATER	BOILED WATER
A	7	5
B	2	2
C	4	4

a) Which river contained the softest water? ....

b) Which river contained the hardest water? ....

c) Why was less soap needed to form a lasting lather after the water from river A was boiled?

....

....

Titration

Q1 Sulfuric acid reacts with sodium hydroxide to form a **neutral** solution.

Xavier wants to find out how much sulfuric acid is needed to **neutralise** a sample of sodium hydroxide. He decides to carry out a **titration**.

a) During the titration, Xavier will need to use an **indicator**. He is planning to use **universal indicator**.

i) Explain why this isn't a suitable indicator to use.

....

....

ii) Suggest one indicator that Xavier could use instead. ....

b) Write out a step-by-step **method** for Xavier to follow for the titration.

....

....

....

....

....

....

....

....

c) Draw and label the **apparatus** he should use in the box below.

Titration Calculations

Q1 Work out the number of **moles** in the following solutions.

Remember, no. of moles = conc. x vol.

a) 1 dm^3 of 2 mol/dm^3 HCl.

....

b) 100 cm^3 of 1 mol/dm^3 NaOH.

....

c) 25 cm^3 of 0.1 mol/dm^3 HNO_3.

....

d) 10 cm^3 of 0.2 mol/dm^3 KOH.

....

Q2 Complete and balance the **symbol equations** for the following acid/alkali reactions.

Hint: acid + alkali → salt + water.

a) **HCl + NaOH →** .... **+** ....

b) **H_2SO_4 +** .... **KOH →** .... **+** ....

Q3 Work out the **masses** and **concentrations** below.

You can look up relative atomic masses in a periodic table — you don't have to learn them.

a) Work out the **mass** of acid or alkali present in each solution below.

i) 0.5 moles of NaOH.

....

ii) 0.2 moles of H_2SO_4.

....

iii) 0.02 moles of $Ca(OH)_2$.

....

b) Work out the concentration in **g/dm^3** of the solutions below.

i) 0.1 mol/dm^3 potassium hydroxide (KOH) solution.

....

ii) 2 mol/dm^3 nitric acid (HNO_3).

....

Titration Calculations

Q4 The concentration of some sodium hydroxide, **NaOH**, was determined by titration with hydrochloric acid, **HCl**. **25 cm³** of NaOH required **20 cm³** of **0.1 mol/dm³** HCl to neutralise it. Work out the concentration of the NaOH in **g/dm³** using the steps outlined below.

a) How many moles of HCl are present in 20 cm³ of 0.1 mol/dm³ solution?

....

b) Complete the equation for this reaction.

.... + ... → NaCl + ...

c) From the equation, ... mole(s) of HCl reacts with .... mole(s) of NaOH.

d) Use your answer to **c)** to work out how many moles of NaOH there are in 25 cm³ of NaOH.

....

e) What is the concentration of the sodium hydroxide in moles per dm³?

....

f) What is the concentration of the sodium hydroxide in grams per dm³?

....

Q5 In a titration, **10 cm³** of **sulfuric acid solution** was used to neutralise **30 cm³** of **0.1 mol/dm³ potassium hydroxide solution**.

$$H_2SO_4 + 2KOH \rightarrow K_2SO_4 + 2H_2O$$

a) **i)** Calculate the number of moles of KOH.

....

ii) Use the equation above to work out how many moles of H_2SO_4 react with the KOH.

....

iii) Calculate the concentration of H_2SO_4 in moles per dm³.

....

b) What is the concentration of the sulfuric acid in grams per dm³?

....

Top Tips: Aargh, calculations. As if Chemistry wasn't tricky enough without maths getting involved too (but at least it's not as bad as Physics). Actually, these aren't the worst calculations as long as you tackle them in stages and know your equations.

Energy

Q1 Use the words to **complete** the blanks in the passage. You can use some words more than once.

endothermic **exothermic** **energy** **heat** **an increase** **a decrease**

All chemical reactions involve changes in .... In .... reactions, ... energy is given out to the surroundings. A thermometer will show .... in temperature.

In .... reactions, ... energy is taken in from the surroundings. A thermometer will show .... in temperature.

Q2 Fiz investigated the **temperature change** during a reaction. She added 25 cm^3 of sodium hydroxide solution to 25 cm^3 of hydrochloric acid. She used a **data logger** to measure the temperature of the reaction over the first **five** seconds.

The data logger records the temperatures automatically.

Fiz plotted her results on the graph shown to the right.

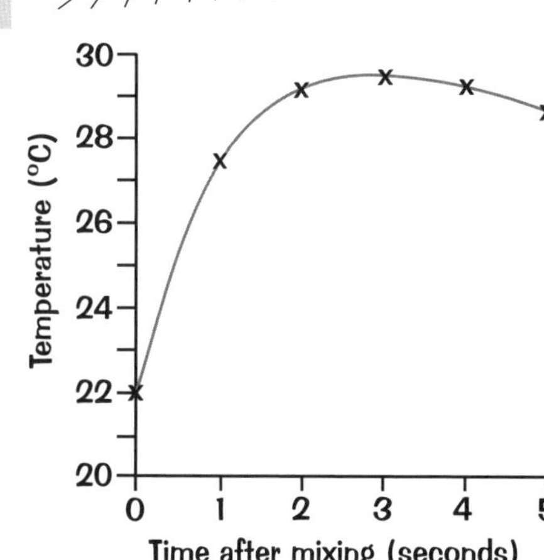

a) What was the increase in temperature due to the reaction?

....

b) Circle any of the words below that correctly describe the reaction in this experiment.

neutralisation **combustion**

endothermic **respiration** **exothermic**

c) Why is it difficult to get **an accurate result** for the temperature change in an experiment like this?

....

Q3 **Circle** the correct words to complete each of the sentences below.

a) Energy must be supplied to **break** / **form** bonds.

b) Energy is released when bonds are **broken** / **formed**.

c) Bond breaking is an **exothermic** / **endothermic** process.

d) Bond forming is an **exothermic** / **endothermic** process.

Q4 During the following reaction the reaction mixture's temperature **increases**.

AB + C → AC + B

a) Is the reaction exothermic or endothermic? ....

b) Which bond is stronger, A–B or A–C? Explain your answer. ....

....

Energy and Fuels

Q1 Answer the following questions on **fuels** and **calorimetry**.

a) Why is **copper** often used as the material for calorimetry cans?

....

b) Why is the experimental energy content of a fuel often much less than the actual energy content?

....

Q2 In a calorimetry experiment, **0.7 g** of petrol raised the temperature of **50 g** of water by **30.5 °C**.

a) Given that it takes **4.2 J** to raise the temperature of **1 g** of water by **1 °C**, calculate the energy transferred to the water.

Use: $Q = mc\Delta T$

....

b) Use your answer to **a)** to calculate the energy produced per gram of petrol. Give your answer in units of **kJ/g**.

....

Q3 A petrol alternative, **fuel X**, has been sent for testing. A scientist tests it using calorimetry. Burning **0.8 g** of fuel X raises the temperature of **50 g** of water by **27 °C**.

a) Calculate the energy produced per gram of fuel X.

....

....

b) Look at your answers to **a)** and **Q2 b)**. Using this evidence only, decide whether petrol or fuel X would make the better fuel. Explain your choice.

....

Q4 There are **environmental** and **economic** consequences of burning fuels.

a) Name the main greenhouse gas released when fossil fuels are burnt. ....

b) Give a possible consequence of increasing levels of greenhouse gases in the atmosphere.

....

c) Explain one potential **economic problem** caused by our reliance on crude oil for fuels.

....

....

....

Bond Energies

Q1 The **energy level diagrams** below represent the energy changes in five chemical reactions.

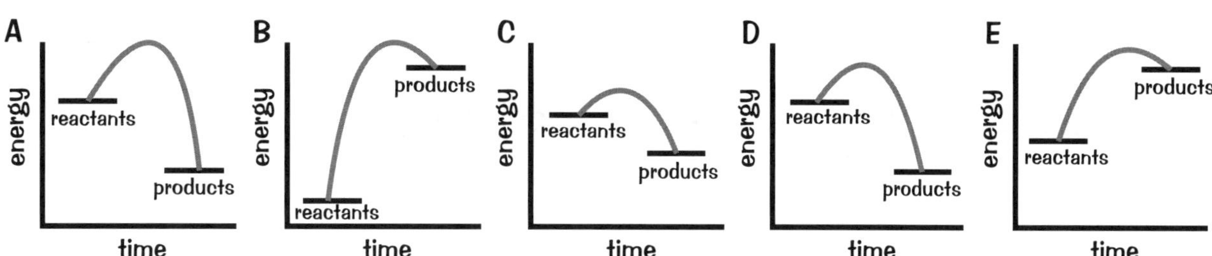

Which diagram(s) show:

a) an exothermic reaction? .... **b)** the reaction with the largest activation energy? ....

c) an endothermic reaction? .... **d)** the reaction with the smallest change in energy? ....

Q2 Answer the following questions about **energy changes**.

a) A chemical reaction has an energy change of +42 kJ/mol.
Is this reaction exothermic or endothermic?

....

b) What is meant by **activation energy**?

....

c) What effect do catalysts have on chemical reactions, and why?

....

....

Q3 To the right is an energy level diagram for a reaction.

a) Give the energy change for the reaction.

....

Remember to show whether your value is +ve or –ve.

b) Give the value of the activation energy.

....

c) Add another energy level diagram to the graph to show the same reaction but with a **catalyst** added.

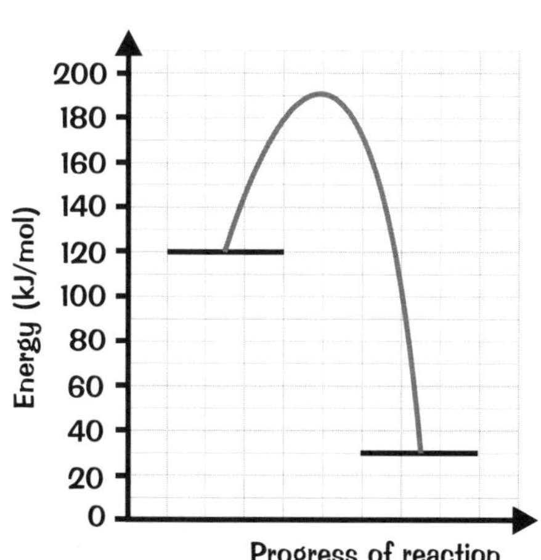

Top Tips: It's easy to mix up the two types of reaction. So just learn this: exothermic = energy given out = negative energy change = energy of products lower than energy of reactants = more energy released in making new bonds than needed for breaking old bonds. That's all there is to it.

Bond Energies

Q4 The equations below show the combustion of **methane**.

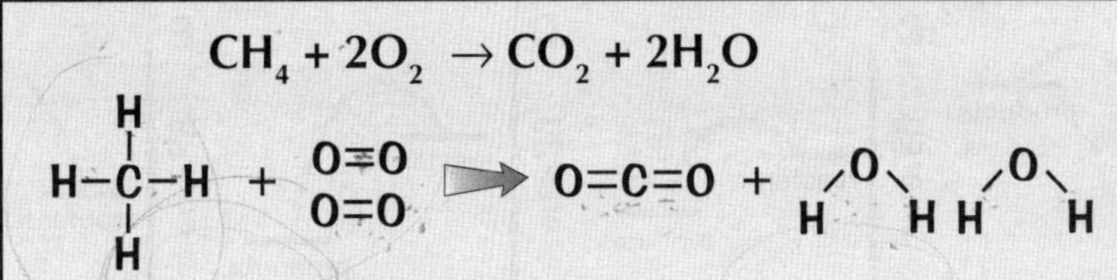

Use the bond energies given below to answer the questions.

C–H = +412 kJ/mol **O=O = +498 kJ/mol** **C=O = +743 kJ/mol** **O–H = +463 kJ/mol**

a) What is the total energy required to break all the bonds in the reactants?

(412 x 4) + (498 x 2) = 1648 + 996 = 2644

Carefully count how many of each type of bond there are.

b) What is the total energy released when the bonds in the products are formed?

(743 x 2) + (463 x 4) = 3338

c) Use your answers to **a)** and **b)** to calculate the energy change for the reaction.

Don't forget to include a '+' or a '–'.

2644 – 3338 = –694 exothermic

Q5 Calculate the energy change for the combustion of hydrazine, N_2H_4.

$$N_2H_4 + O_2 \rightarrow N_2 + 2H_2O$$

H₂N–NH₂ + O=O → N≡N + H–O–H H–O–H

N–N = +158 kJ/mol
N≡N = +945 kJ/mol
N–H = +391 kJ/mol

Use the bond energies above and those given in **Q4**.

....

....

Q6 Calculate the energy change for the combustion of ethane.

$$2C_2H_6 + 7O_2 \rightarrow 4CO_2 + 6H_2O$$

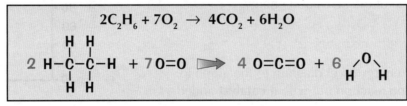

2 H₃C–CH₃ + 7 O=O → 4 O=C=O + 6 H–O–H

Use the bond energies given in **Q4**, and **C–C = +348 kJ/mol**.

....

....

Getting Energy from Hydrogen

Q1 Hydrogen and oxygen react together in an **exothermic** reaction.

a) What is the only product when hydrogen and oxygen react together? ....

b) Hydrogen can be burned in oxygen in an internal combustion engine to power a car.

i) Give **one advantage** of using hydrogen in this way.

....

ii) Give **one disadvantage** of using hydrogen in this way.

....

Q2 Fill in the blanks to complete the passage below.

A fuel cell is an electrical cell that's supplied with a .... and .... and uses energy from the reaction between them to generate ....

Q3 Cars are being developed that run on fuel cells.

Explain how using these cars could help reduce the amount of air pollution in cities.

....

....

....

Q4 Explain why hydrogen fuel cells are unlikely to mean the end of our dependence on fossil fuels.

....

....

....

....

Tests for Positive Ions

Q1 **Flame tests** are often carried out to identify unknown substances.

a) Complete the statement about **positive ions** below by circling the correct word.

Metals always / don't always form positive ions.

b) Describe how you would use a wire loop to carry out a flame test on an unknown powder.

....

....

....

c) Suggest why the results of this test would be unreliable if the wire loop used had not been cleaned properly.

....

Q2 Les had five samples of **metal compounds**. He tested each one using a flame test.

a) Draw lines to match each of Les's observations to the positive metal ion producing the coloured flame.

red flame	Na^+
yellow flame	Ba^{2+}
crimson flame	K^+
green flame	Ca^{2+}
lilac flame	Li^+

b) Les wants to recommend a compound to use in a firework at a fundraising event for his local football team. Which of the following compounds should he recommend in order for the firework to explode in his team's colour, lilac? Circle your answer.

silver nitrate **sodium chloride** **barium sulfate**

potassium nitrate **calcium carbonate**

Top Tips: Right, this stuff needs to be learnt, and learnt properly. Otherwise you'll be stuck in your exam staring at a question about coloured flames and there won't be any sparks upstairs. That's a grim thought. So, snap out of it, think positive, and get learning the science behind the pretty fireworks.

Tests for Positive Ions

Q3 Cilla adds a few drops of **NaOH** solution to solutions of different **metal compounds**.

a) Complete her table of results.

Positive Ion	Colour of Precipitate
Fe^{2+}	
	blue
Fe^{3+}	
Al^{3+}	

b) Complete the balanced ionic equation for the reaction of iron(II) ions with hydroxide ions.

$Fe^{2+}_{(............)}$ + ... $OH^{-}_{(aq)}$ → ....$_{(s)}$

c) Write a balanced ionic equation for the reaction of **iron(III) ions** with hydroxide ions. Include state symbols.

....

d) Cilla adds a few drops of sodium hydroxide solution to **aluminium sulfate solution**. She continues adding sodium hydroxide to excess. What would she observe at each stage?

....

....

Q4 Select compounds from the box to match the following statements.

KCl	LiCl	$FeSO_4$	$FeCl_3$	$Al_2(SO_4)_3$
NaCl	$CuSO_4$	$CaCl_2$	$MgCl_2$	$BaCl_2$

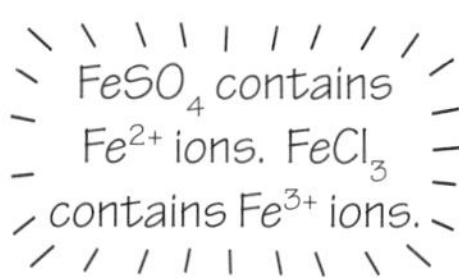

$FeSO_4$ contains Fe^{2+} ions. $FeCl_3$ contains Fe^{3+} ions.

a) This compound forms a blue precipitate with sodium hydroxide solution. ....

b) This compound gives a crimson flame in a flame test. ....

c) This compound forms a white precipitate with sodium hydroxide **that dissolves if excess sodium hydroxide is added.** ....

d) This compound forms a green precipitate with sodium hydroxide solution. ....

e) This compound forms a brown precipitate with sodium hydroxide solution. ....

f) This compound reacts with sodium hydroxide to form a white precipitate, **and it also gives a red flame in a flame test.** ....

Tests for Negative Ions

Q1 Give the chemical formula and charge of the **negative ions** present in the following compounds.

a) barium sulfate ....

b) potassium iodide ....

c) magnesium carbonate ....

Q2 Use the words given to complete the passage below.

carbon dioxide	alkali	limewater	acid	hydrogen

A test for the presence of carbonates in an unidentified substance involves reacting it with dilute .... If carbonates are present then .... will be formed. You can test for this by bubbling it through .... to see if it becomes milky.

Q3 Answer the following questions on testing for **sulfate ions**.

a) Which two reactants are used to test for sulfate ions?

....

b) What would you see after adding these reactants to a sulfate compound?

....

Q4 Deirdre wants to find out if a soluble compound contains **chloride**, **bromide** or **iodide ions**. Explain how she could do this.

....

....

....

Q5 Complete the following symbol equations for reactions involved in **negative ion** tests.

a) $Ag^{+}_{(aq)}$ + ... → $AgCl_{(s)}$

b) $2HCl_{(aq)} + Na_2CO_{3(s)} \rightarrow 2NaCl_{(aq)}$ + ...$_{(l)}$ + ...$_{(g)}$

c) .... + ... → $BaSO_{4(s)}$

Mixed Questions — Chemistry 3b

Q1 **Aerobic respiration** is the process of breaking down food using oxygen to release energy.

sugar + oxygen → carbon dioxide + water + energy

a) Is this an **exothermic** or an **endothermic** reaction? Explain your answer.

....

b) Choose the correct words to complete this statement about the above equation.

> The energy needed to **break** the bonds in the reactants is **greater than / less than** the energy released when the bonds in the products are **formed**.

c) Describe one method that could be used to find the amount of energy in a food or a fuel.

....

....

d) A 0.5 g sample of sugar is burned and releases enough energy to raise the temperature of 100 g of water by 15 °C. Calculate the energy produced per gram of sugar.

Use: $Q = mc\Delta T$. The specific heat capacity of water is 4.2 J.

....

....

Q2 Stanley is trying to identify a mystery substance.

First he adds a few drops of sodium hydroxide solution to a solution of the mystery compound.

a) What result would you expect Stanley to see if the mystery compound contained Fe^{2+} ions?

....

...and add a splash of
$CaSO_4$, with a dollop
of $MgBr_2$ and a dash of
Worcester sauce...

b) In fact, a blue precipitate forms. What can Stanley conclude?

....

c) Write down an **ionic equation** for the formation of this blue precipitate.

....

d) Stanley suspects that his compound is a sulfate. Describe a test he could do to see if he's right.

....

....

e) Stanley does the test for a sulfate, and sees a white precipitate form in the solution.

Write down the formula of Stanley's mystery compound. ....

Mixed Questions — Chemistry 3b

Q3 The diagram shows the progress of a reaction which was carried out twice, once with a **catalyst** and once without.

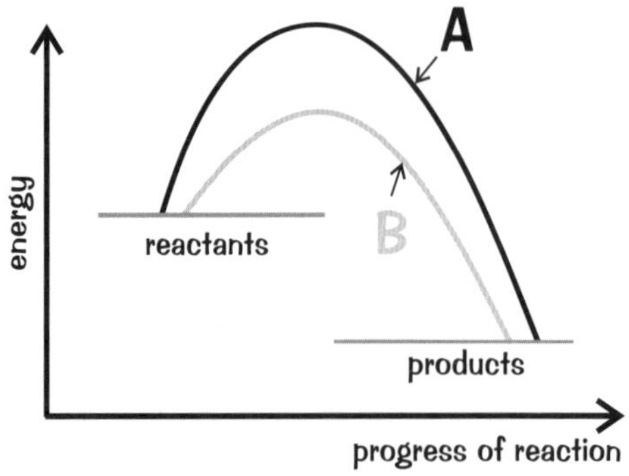

a) Label the **overall energy change** of the reaction with the symbol ΔH.

b) Label the activation energy for reaction B on the graph.

c) Which reaction used a **catalyst**, A or B? ....

d) Does the graph represent an exothermic or an endothermic reaction?

....

Q4 Which ions would give the following results?

a) Red colour in a flame test. ....

b) Releases a gas that turns limewater cloudy when added to an acid. ....

c) Forms a brown precipitate when NaOH solution is added. ....

d) Forms a white precipitate after dilute HCl followed by $BaCl_2$ is added. ....

Q5 During a titration, 20 cm^3 of 0.5 mol/dm^3 sodium hydroxide solution was used to neutralise 25 cm^3 of hydrochloric acid.

a) In a titration experiment, suggest an **indicator** to use with HCl.

....

b) What is the **concentration** of the acid, in:

i) moles per dm^3?

....

....

....

....

ii) grams per dm^3?

....

....

....

X-rays in Medicine

Q1 In each of the following sentences, circle the correct word(s) from each highlighted pair.

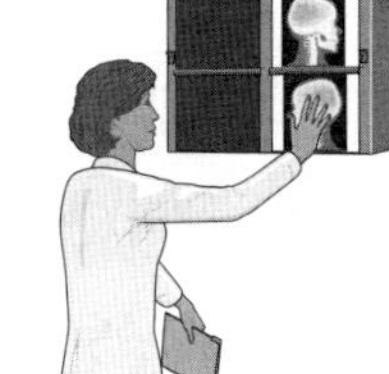

a) X-rays are **short / long** wavelength electromagnetic waves that can cause **refraction / ionisation**.

b) X-rays are **transmitted / absorbed** by healthy soft tissue but are **transmitted / absorbed** by dense materials such as bone.

c) Electronic images can be formed using a **photographic film / charge-coupled device**.

d) The wavelength of an X-ray is roughly the same as the diameter of a **car / cell / atom**.

Q2 Complete the following paragraph using the words provided.

ill	centre	normal	kill	cells	focused	cancer	rotating

High doses of X-ray radiation will .... living .... Because of this, X-rays are used to treat .... X-rays are .... on the tumour using a wide beam. Damage to .... cells can make the patient feel very .... This damage is minimised by .... the X-ray beam, keeping the tumour at the ....

Q3 X-ray images can be used to **diagnose** medical conditions.

a) Describe how X-ray images can be formed using **photographic film**.

....

....

....

....

b) Briefly describe how X-ray images can be formed **electronically**.

....

....

....

c) Name one medical condition that X-rays can be used to diagnose.

....

X-rays in Medicine

Q4 Tick the boxes to show whether each of these statements is **true** or **false**.

		True	False
a)	The images created using CT scans have a high resolution.	☐	☐
b)	Only soft tissue can be imaged by CT scans.	☐	☐
c)	CT scans use less X-ray radiation than traditional X-ray imaging.	☐	☐
d)	A drawback of CT scanning is its use of ionising radiation.	☐	☐

Q5 When a CT scan is taken, an image is produced by a computer. Order the statements below 1 to 5 to describe the process of taking a CT scan. The first one has been done for you.

☐ An X-ray tube emits an X-ray beam whilst rotating around the patient.

☐ Multiple slice images are put together to give a three-dimensional picture.

☐ A computer uses the detected X-rays to generate an image of a two-dimensional slice through the body.

☐ Detectors on the opposite side of the scanner measure the intensity of transmitted X-rays.

1 The patient is put inside the CT scanner.

Q6 When radiographers take X-ray 'photographs' or scans of patients, they themselves are exposed to X-rays.

a) Write down **two precautions** radiographers can take to minimise their exposure to X-rays.

1. ....

2. ....

b) Describe **two** ways in which the patient's radiation dose can be **minimised**.

1. ....

....

2. ....

....

Top Tips: In a CT scan, the image is built up by the subtle differences in different tissues' ability to block the X-ray beam. Because lots of 2D 'slice' images are created, there's no problem of different body parts getting in the way of each other like there is in an X-ray — you get the complete picture.

Ultrasound

Q1 Ultrasound imaging can be used to diagnose soft tissue problems.

a) What is ultrasound?

....

b) How can ultrasound of a particular frequency be generated?

....

....

Q2 Ultrasound can be used to detect the existence of a different medium below the surface of an object, and to measure how far below the surface it is.

Sketch a diagram showing what happens when an ultrasound wave hits the boundary between one medium and another.

Q3 A layer of **fat** sitting between a layer of **skin** and a layer of **muscle** is examined using **ultrasound**. The **oscilloscope trace** below shows two pulses of ultrasound from the examination — the first pulse is reflected off the layer of fat and the second is reflected off the layer of muscle. Each **time division** on the oscilloscope represents **5 μs** and the speed of sound through tissue is **1450 m/s**.

a) Calculate the distance from the ultrasound device to the layer of fat.

1 μs = 0.000001 s

....

....

....

b) Use the oscilloscope trace to calculate the **thickness of the layer of fat**. Give your answer in centimetres and to one decimal place.

....

....

....

Ultrasound Uses

Q1 A concentrated beam of **ultrasound** can be used to treat kidney stones.

a) What effect does the ultrasound beam have on kidney stones?

....

b) How are the kidney stone remains removed from the body?

....

c) Give two reasons why using ultrasound is a good way of treating kidney stones.

1. ....

2. ....

Q2 Doctors use different imaging techniques to diagnose different medical conditions.

a) Fill in the table below with **one advantage** and **one disadvantage** of ultrasound, X-rays and CT scans.

	Advantage	Disadvantage
Ultrasound imaging		
X-ray photographs		
CT scans		

b) Which medical imaging technique would you recommend for the planning of complicated brain surgery? Explain your answer

....

....

Q3 Ultrasound can be used in a similar way to **X-rays**.

a) Why is ultrasound safer than X-rays?

....

b) State whether X-rays or ultrasound would be used to investigate a suspected broken bone, and explain why.

....

....

....

Refractive Index

Q1 The diagram below shows light entering a glass block.

a) As the light enters the glass block it changes direction. What is the name of this effect?

....

b) Complete the diagram to show the ray passing through the block and emerging from the other side. Include labels A to E for:

- **A** the refracted ray
- **B** the emergent ray
- **C** the normal for the emergent ray
- **D** the angle of incidence
- **E** the angle of refraction

Q2 Every transparent material has a refractive index.

a) What is refractive index?

....

b) Write down the equation that connects refractive index, angle of incidence and angle of refraction.

....

Q3 A light ray was shone from air into some water. The ray had an **angle of incidence** of **30°** and an **angle of refraction** of **22°**. Use this data to calculate the **refractive index** of water.

....

....

Q4 The diagram shows light when it refracts from **air** into **glass**. The refractive index of the glass is 1.514. Calculate the **angle of refraction** for the incident light.

....

....

....

....

Lenses and Images

Q1 Lenses can be either **converging** or **diverging**.

a) In the following sentences the words **parallel**, **converging**, **principal focus** and **incident** have been replaced by the letters **W**, **X**, **Y**, **Z**. Write down which words are represented by **W**, **X**, **Y** and **Z**.

*A **W** ray passing through the centre of an **X** lens from any angle carries on in the same direction.*

*An **X** lens causes all **W** rays **Y** to the axis to meet at the **Z**.*

*An **X** lens causes all **W** rays passing through the **Z** to emerge **Y** to the axis.*

W .... **X** .... **Y** .... **Z** ....

b) Which of the following incident rays do not have their direction changed by either type of lens? Tick any boxes which apply.

- ☐ Any ray parallel to the axis
- ☐ Any ray passing through the centre of the lens
- ☐ Any ray passing along the axis
- ☐ Any ray passing through the principal focus

Q2 Tick the boxes to show whether each of these statements is **true** or **false**.

		True	False
a)	Only diverging lenses can produce a virtual image.	☐	☐
b)	The focal length of a lens is the distance from the centre of the lens to the principal focus.	☐	☐
c)	A real image can be projected on a screen	☐	☐
d)	A converging lens is concave.	☐	☐

Q3 In the ray diagrams below, the pictures of the lenses have been removed.

a) What type of lens could this be? Underline the correct answer from the options below.

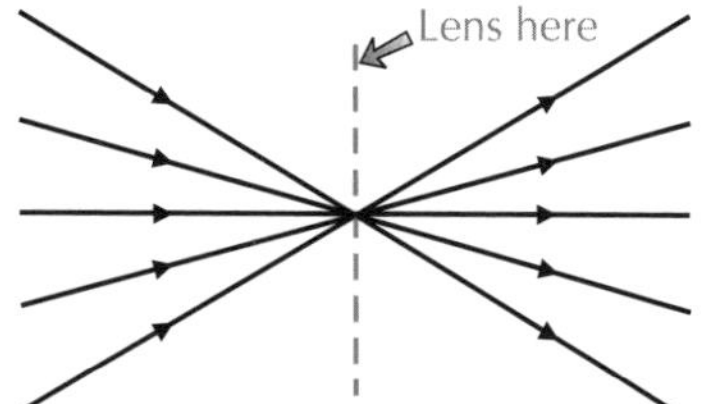

A A converging lens

B A diverging lens

C Neither a converging nor a diverging lens

D Either a converging or a diverging lens

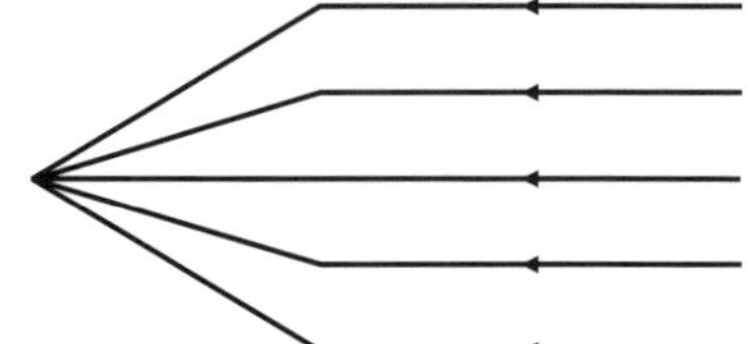

b) On the diagram to the right, draw a lens of the correct type in the right position to complete the ray diagram.

Top Tips: It may look like we've diverged away from medicine, but fear not, we shall converge on it again in a few pages when we look at what lenses are used for. If you can't guess what I'm talking about, here's a little hint — you almost certainly know someone who wears a pair (and they aren't pants).

Lenses and Images

Q4 Images formed by lenses can either be **real** or **virtual**.

a) What is the difference between a real and a virtual image?

....

....

b) What **three** pieces of information do you need to give to describe the nature of an image?

1. ....

2. ....

3. ....

Q5 This question is about how to **draw ray diagrams** for **converging lenses**.

a) The first step is to draw a ray from the **top** of the object going **parallel** to the **axis** of the lens. Where does this ray pass through when it's refracted?

....

b) The next step is to draw a ray from the top of the object which passes through the lens **without** being refracted. Where does this ray pass through the lens?

....

c) How do the steps above tell you where the **top** of the **image** will be on the ray diagram?

....

Q6 The diagram shows a **diverging lens**.

a) Draw the path of a ray passing through the lens **along the axis** from left to right.

b) Draw the paths of two incident rays **parallel** to the first ray, one **above** and one **below** the axis.

c) Sketch in the position of the **virtual principal focus** for the rays shown and label it "F".

Lenses

Q1 Some of this diagram has been hidden. Draw in the rest of the diagram, showing the position of the **object** that produced the image you see.

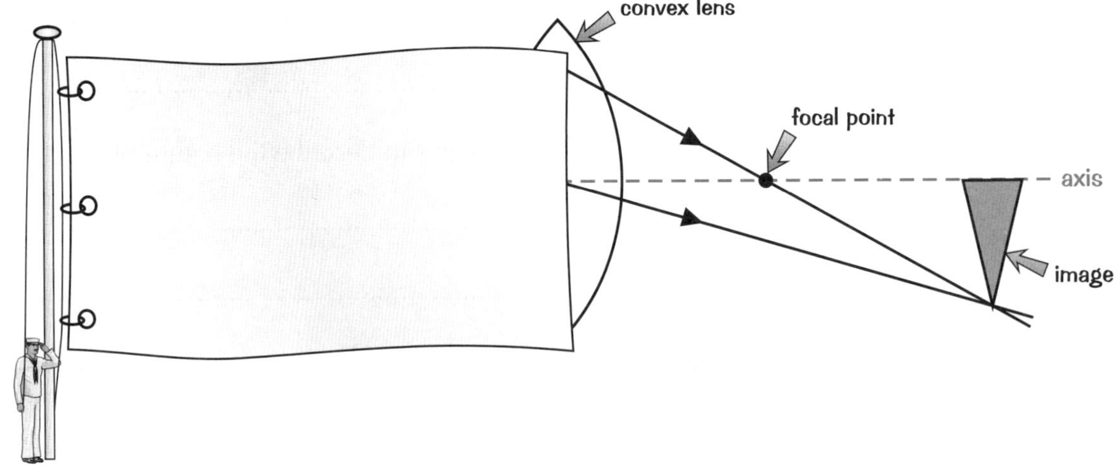

Q2 Circle the correct options in this description of images formed by **diverging lenses**.

Diverging lenses always produce **real / virtual**, **upright / inverted** images which are **smaller / larger** than the object.

Q3 The table below gives information about the images formed by a **converging lens** when the object is at different positions, where F is the principal focus of the lens.

Distance from lens to object	Distance from lens to image	Type of image	Size of image
Greater than 2F	Between 2F and F	Real, inverted	Smaller than object
Equal to 2F		Real, inverted	
Between 2F and F	Greater than 2F		
Less than F	Greater than 2F		Larger than object

a) Fill in the blanks in the table.

b) An object has a height of 1 cm. It stands on the axis of a converging lens, 5 cm away from it. The focal length of the lens (distance from the lens to the principal focus) is 2.5 cm.

i) What size will the image be?

....

ii) Where will the image be formed, relative to the lens and the object?

....

Lenses

Q4 An aubergine is placed **6.1 cm** away from a converging lens with a focal length of **7 cm**.

a) Will the image formed by the lens be:

i) upright or inverted? ....

ii) on the same side of the lens or on the opposite side? ....

iii) real or virtual? ....

b) The aubergine is now placed at a distance x from the lens. The image is now bigger than the object and inverted. Which of the options below could be distance x? Circle your answer.

A 3.9 cm **B 7.0 cm** **C 10.2 cm** **D 14.0 cm** **E 15.3 cm**

Q5 The diagram below shows an object placed next to a diverging lens. The locations of each principal focus are marked F.

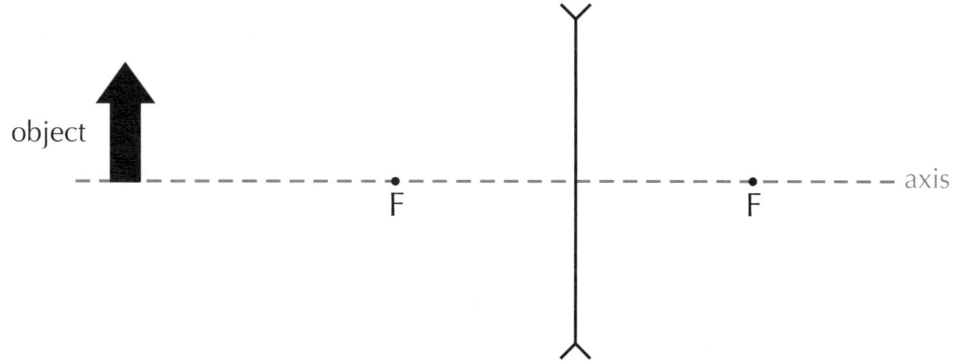

a) On the diagram, draw the path of a ray coming from the top of the object and travelling in the direction of the centre of the lens.

b) Draw the path of a ray coming from the top of the object and going towards the lens parallel to the axis.

c) Draw the image formed by the lens.

Q6 Complete the ray diagram below to show the image produced by the lens.

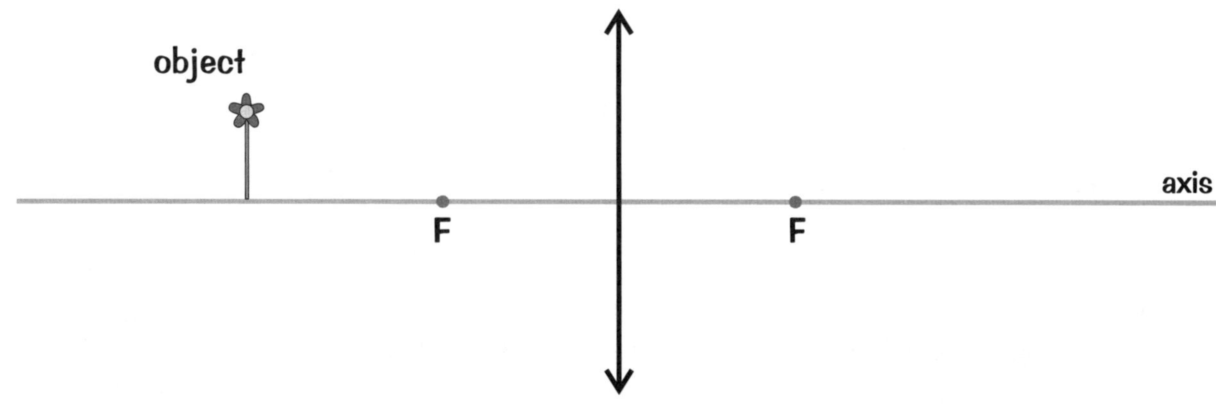

Top Tips: Aubergines aside, you'll be expected to know how to draw lovely ray diagrams for converging and diverging lenses. They can be a bit tricky, but examiners love 'em, so get practising.

Magnification and Power

Q1 Mr Richards is using a **magnifying glass** to read a magazine by the light of an overhead lamp.

a) What sort of lens is used in a magnifying glass?

....

b) Explain why an object you want to view with a magnifying glass must be placed nearer to the lens than the principal focus.

....

....

c) The writing on the magazine is in focus when the lens is a distance of 9 cm or less from the magazine. When the magnifying glass is held exactly 26 cm from the magazine a sharply focused image of the light bulb appears on the magazine.

Three of the following statements are **true**. Circle the appropriate letters.

A	The lens works as a magnifying glass when it is held anywhere nearer than 26 cm to the magazine.
B	The lens works as a magnifying glass when it is held anywhere nearer than 9 cm to the magazine.
C	The focal length of the lens is 26 cm.
D	The focal length of the lens is 9 cm.
E	The image of the light bulb projected onto the magazine is a real image.
F	The image of the light bulb projected onto the magazine is a virtual image.

Q2 The magnification of a magnifying glass depends on the distance of the object from the lens.

a) State the formula for the magnification produced by a lens or mirror.

....

b) A handwriting expert is studying a handwritten letter "A" with a magnifying glass. The letter is 0.5 cm high. When a magnifying glass is held 10 cm from the letter, the image of the letter appears to be 0.8 cm high. What is the magnification of the glass at that distance?

....

c) The same magnifying glass is used to look at a ring made from a strip of gold of width 3 mm. The ring is also held 10 cm from the glass. How wide will the image be?

....

heh
heh
heh...

Magnification and Power

Q3 Convex lenses can also be called **converging lenses**.

a) Which lenses are more powerful? Circle the correct answer.

thinner lenses fatter lenses

b) Write out the equation that relates lens power to focal length.

....

Q4 Dave is using a converging lens to **focus** some parallel rays of light to a point.

X Y

a) If the distance between the centre of the lens, X, and the principal focus, Y, is 15 cm, what is the power of the lens?

....

b) Dave wants to increase the distance between the lens and the principal focus, so he switches the lens for one with a power of 5.2 D. Calculate the new distance between X and Y.

....

c) How is the power of a **diverging** lens different to that of a **converging** lens?

....

Q5 Nanny Irene goes to the opticians to get some new glasses.

a) What **two** factors determine the focal length of a lens?

1. ....

2. ....

b) Despite the focal length of her eyes staying the same, Nanny Irene gets new glasses with **thinner** lenses than before. Explain how the manufacturers of her glasses achieved this.

....

....

....

The Eye

Q1 Add labels to complete the diagram of the eye below.

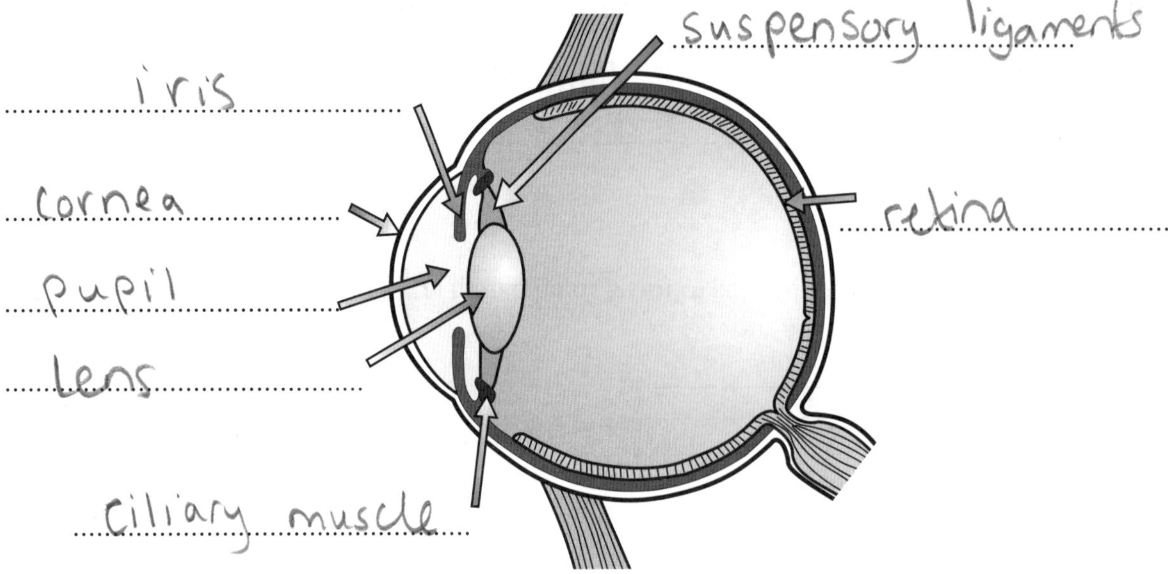

Q2 Tuan is photographing a football match for his school magazine.

a) How is the image produced in a camera similar to the image produced in a human eye?

the image is real and inverted.

b) Explain why Tuan can't take a picture of an object closer than the focal length of the camera lens.

....

....

c) Circle the correct words or phrases from the alternatives given in the following passage.

For the photograph not to be blurred the image must be formed **at the lens / between the lens and the film / on the film.** The image formed is **smaller / bigger** than the object being photographed because the object is further than the focal length of the lens. The film (or CCD) in the camera is the equivalent to the **pupil / retina** in the eye.

Top Tips: Make sure you can label that diagram correctly and have a good understanding of what all the different parts of the eye do — it's the sort of thing that could turn up in an exam all too easily...

The Eye

Q3 **Complete the table** about the functions of different parts of the eye.

Part of the eye	Function
Cornea	Focuses light on the retina
Retina	detects light and send signals to the brain
Ciliary muscles	Contracts and relaxs to change the lens.
pupil	Hole through which light enters the eye

Q4 Circle the correct word in each pair to complete the passage below.

When you look at distant objects, your ciliary muscles **contract** / **relax**, and pull the lens to make it **thin** / **fat**. The opposite actions happen when you look at near objects. The combined action of the lens and **cornea** / **iris** focuses the light on the **pupil** / **retina** to produce an image. Cells on the **pupil** / **retina** send signals to the brain to be interpreted via the optic nerve.

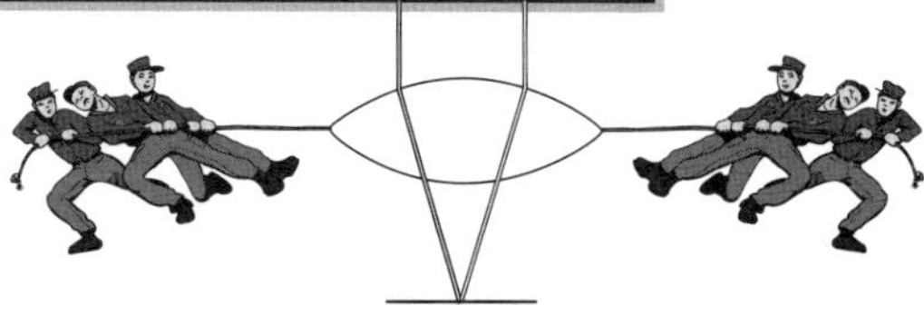

Q5 The range of human eyesight lies between the **near** and **far points**. Complete the definitions of near and far points below.

a) The near point is the closest distance that the eye can focus on.

For normally-sighted adults, the near point is about 25 cm.

b) The far point is the furthest distance that the eye can focus comfortably.

For normally-sighted adults, the far point is at infinity.

Correcting Vision

Q1 Common vision problems are caused by the eye focusing an image in the wrong place.

a) Look at the image on the right. Complete the sentences by choosing the correct word(s) from the highlighted options.

The person with this vision defect is **short / long** sighted.

The **near / far** point is closer than infinity, which makes it difficult to focus on things that are **close up / far away**. The object in the diagram is brought into focus **in front of / behind** the retina.

object

b) Give **two** possible causes of the problem shown in the diagram.

1. ....

2. ....

c) **i)** Which of the two lenses shown on the right could correct this problem? Circle the correct letter.

A B

ii) Explain how the lens you chose in part **c)i)** would help to correct the eye problem.

....

....

....

Q2 **Lasers** are increasingly used in surgery.

a) What is a laser?

....

b) Lasers can cut, cauterise and burn tissue.

i) Explain what cauterisation means.

....

ii) Briefly describe how a surgeon can use a laser to correct long or short sight.

....

....

....

Top Tips: Corrective lenses can be in the form of spectacles **or** contact lenses — which ones you wear is up to you. Remember, both can be either diverging or converging lenses. Good 'ol lenses.

Total Internal Reflection

Q1 Doctors can use an **endoscope**, a thin tube containing **optical fibres**, to look inside a patient's body.

Light source

Endoscope

a) What type of radiation is sent along optical fibres?

....

b) What material could the optical fibres in the endoscope be made from?

....

c) Explain why endoscopes contain two bundles of optical fibres.

....

....

d) Optical fibres work because of repeated **total internal reflections**.
Complete the ray diagrams below. The critical angle for glass/air is 42°.

air

glass

air

glass

You'll need to measure the angle of incidence for each one — carefully.

Q2 Martin wants to buy a ring for Marion. He compares a **diamond** ring with a **glass** imitation ring.

a) The critical angle between glass and air is **42°**. Calculate the refractive index of glass.

....

b) Martin knows that the refractive index of diamond is **2.4**.
Calculate the critical angle between diamond and air.

....

c) The glass imitation ring is cut in exactly the same way as the diamond ring.
Which of the two rings will be the most **sparkly**?
Explain your answer using your answers from parts **a)** and **b)**.

Think about how much light will be reflected.

....

....

....

....

Mixed Questions — Physics 3a

Q1 Lara is having a great time investigating how light travels through media.

a) Lara shines a ray of light passing across the **boundary** between two media.

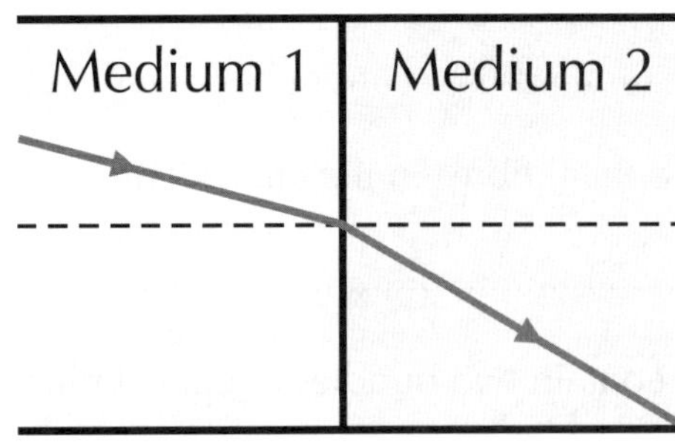

i) Which of Medium 1 and Medium 2 is air and which is glass?

Medium 1 is .... **Medium 2 is** ....

ii) Explain your answer to **a) i)**. ....

....

....

b) i) In which of these situations could Lara get total internal reflection? Circle the correct letter(s).

A Light is travelling from air into water.
B Light is travelling from glass into air.

ii) Explain your answer to **b) i)**. ....

....

....

c) Lara investigates refraction of light in water by shining a beam of light **up** through a fish tank to the air above. She finds the **critical angle** of light travelling from water into air is **49°**.

i) Calculate the refractive index of water.

....

....

ii) She shines the beam of light down into the water from the air at an angle of 20°. Use your answer from part **c) i)** to calculate the angle of refraction of the light.

....

....

....

Mixed Questions — Physics 3a

Q2 Andrew and Cassie are looking at a shell.
They can see it because images **form on their retinas**.

a) Complete the paths of the light rays on the diagram below so that the image of the shell is correctly brought into focus on the retina.

b) The light entering Cassie's eye is shown in the diagram to the right. Her lens is working correctly.

Circle the correct words to complete the sentences below.

Cassie's eyeball is too **long / short,** so images form **behind / in front of** her retina.

This can be corrected by **concave / convex** spectacle lenses as these make light rays converge.

c) Cassie wears glasses to correct her vision.
The lens for her right eye has a focal length of **0.4 m**.

i) Calculate the **power** of the lens.

....

ii) The lens for her left eye is made of the **same material** as the lens for her right eye, but has a **higher power**. Describe how the two lenses will differ in appearance.

....

d) Andrew uses a **magnifying glass** to examine the shell, which is **1.8 cm** tall.
He finds that to magnify the shell, he must hold the lens less than **3 cm** from it.
When he holds the magnifying glass **2.5 cm** away from the shell, the image formed is **4 cm** tall.

i) What is the focal length of this lens?

....

ii) What is the magnification of the lens at 2.5 cm?

....

iii) Is the image real or virtual? Explain your answer.

....

....

Mixed Questions — Physics 3a

Q3 **Ultrasound imaging** is a valuable technique in many different medical investigations.

a) A pulse of ultrasound is directed toward an unborn fetus. It **partially reflects** when it reaches the amniotic fluid and again when it reaches the body of the fetus. An oscilloscope trace shows that the time between the reflected pulses is **26 μs**. The speed of sound through the fluid is 1500 m/s. Calculate how far the fetus is from the outside of the amniotic fluid.

Remember — when something is reflected, the distance it has travelled is there and back.

b) Explain why ultrasound is used in pre-natal scans instead of X-rays.

c) X-rays can be used to treat cancer, but ultrasound can't. Explain why.

d) CT scans can produce very clear images of inside the body, but doctors always try to keep their use to an absolute minimum. Explain why doctors will only take CT scans when it is absolutely necessary.

e) Describe the process of producing a **three-dimensional CT image**. Include the words in the box below in your answer.

X-ray tube	slice	detectors	rotated	computer

Top Tips: Examiners love to ask questions that get you to show that you really know what you're talking about — and a good example is getting you to compare the different medical imaging processes. Make sure you are totally clued up on the pros and cons of X-rays, ultrasound and CT scans.

Turning Forces and the Centre of Mass

Q1 a) Fill in the blanks in the following passage, using the words supplied.

pivot	perpendicular	moment	force

The turning effect of a .... is called its ....
It can be found by multiplying the force by the .... distance from the line of action of the force to the ....

b) What are the units in which moments are measured? ....

Q2 To open a door, its handle needs to be **rotated clockwise**.

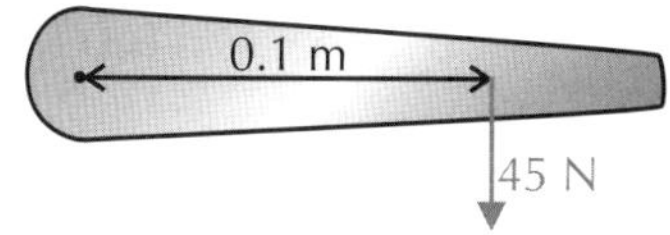

a) A force of 45 N is exerted vertically downwards on the door-handle at a distance of 0.1 m from the pivot. What is the **moment** of the force?

....

b) Pictures **A**, **B**, **C** and **D** show equal forces being exerted on the handle.

A

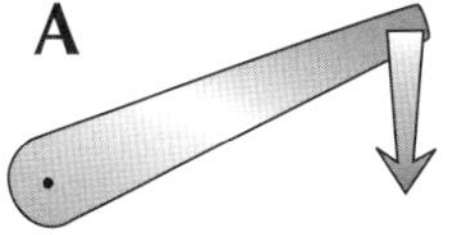

B

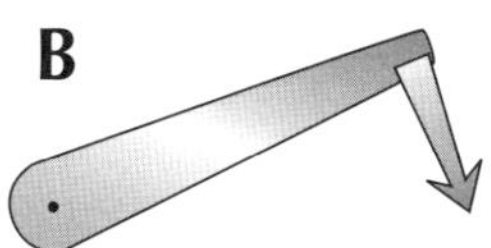

C

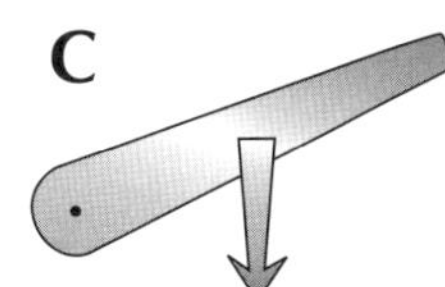

D

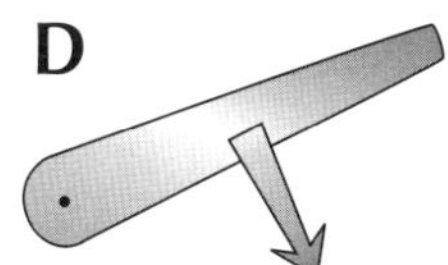

Which of the forces shown (**A**, **B**, **C** or **D**) exerts:

i) the largest moment? .... **ii)** the smallest moment? ....

Q3 A baby's pram toy consists of a toy banana hanging from a bar over the pram.

a) The banana is hanging **at rest**, as shown.
Draw a line on which the centre of mass **must** fall.

b) Complete the following sentences by choosing from the words and phrases below:

level with	vertically below	perpendicular	moment	centre of mass	horizontal

When a suspended object's .... is .... the pivot, the .... distance between the line of action of the gravitational force and the pivot is zero. This means that there is no .... due to the object's weight.

Turning Forces and the Centre of Mass

Q4 You can think of the **centre of mass** as the point where all the mass of an object seems to be concentrated.

a) Using lines of symmetry, find the centre of mass of each of these shapes:

b) **Circle** the correct answer to complete this sentence.
The centre of mass of a raindrop is:

A at the top

B near the top

C midway down

D near the bottom

E at the bottom

Q5 Two men, one at each end, hold a 0.8 m long metal pole weighing 130 N so that it is in a **horizontal** position. One man accidentally lets go of his end.

First, find the centre of mass of the pole.

What is the moment on the pole due to its weight an instant after he lets go?

Draw a diagram.

....

....

....

Q6 Some pupils want to find the centre of mass of an **irregularly shaped** piece of cardboard. They are equipped with a stand to hang the card from, a plumb line and a pencil. They make a hole near one edge of the card and hang it from the stand.

a) What steps should they take next in order to find the centre of mass?

....

....

....

....

b) How could they make their result more reliable?

....

....

Balanced Moments and Levers

Q1 A 2 N weight (Weight A) sits 20 cm to the left of the pivot of a balance.
A 5 N weight (Weight B) is placed 16 cm to the left of the pivot.

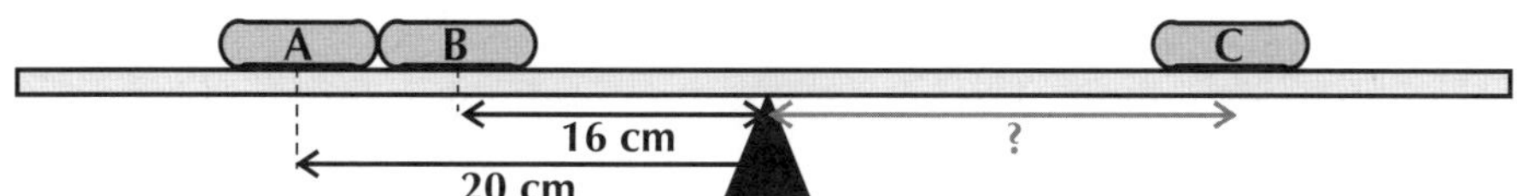

a) What is the moment exerted by **Weight A**? ....

b) What is the moment exerted by **Weight B**? ....

c) How far to the right of the pivot should Weight C (8 N) be placed to **balance** A and B?

....

....

d) If all three of the weights were exactly **twice as far** away from the pivot, would the balance tip over to one side? Explain your answer.

....

Q2 Barbara uses a wheelbarrow to move things around her allotment.
She says "I love my wheelbarrow. It makes it so much easier to lift everything."

Explain **how** a wheelbarrow reduces the amount of force needed to lift an object.

Hint: a wheelbarrow is just a type of lever.

....

....

....

....

....

Q3 One side of a drop-leaf table is pivoted on a hinge and supported 5 cm from its edge by a table leg. The table leaf is 80 cm long and weighs 40 N.

Find the force, F, exerted by the table leg (when the table leaf is fully extended).

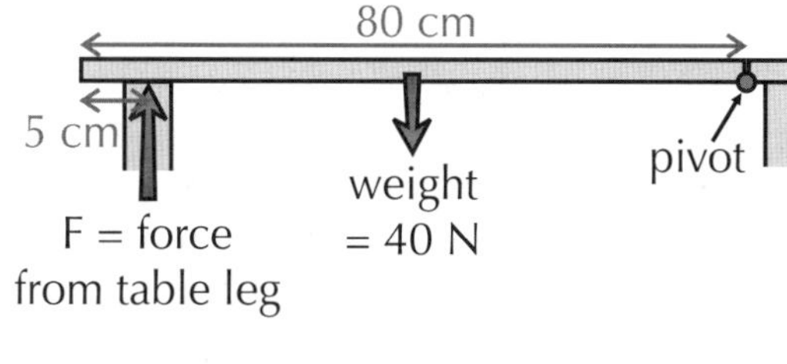

....

....

....

Moments, Stability and Pendulums

Q1 The top drawer of a two-drawer filing cabinet is full of heavy files, but the bottom drawer is empty.

Why is the cabinet in danger of falling over if the top drawer is fully pulled out?

....

....

....

Q2 The pictures show three different designs for **vases**.

A B C

Which vase will be **most stable**? Explain your answer.

....

....

Q3 The diagram to the right shows a cart being used to carry coal along a slope. The centre of mass of the cart, when full, is shown.

Centre of mass

a) Explain why the cart **doesn't** topple over when on the slope.

....

....

b) Suggest **one** way in which the stability of the cart could be improved.

....

Q4 A magician is using a pendulum to practise hypnotism. The pendulum swings with a time period of 1.25 s.

a) Calculate the frequency of the pendulum.

....

....

b) The magician decides the time period of the pendulum's swing needs to be longer to work best. Suggest **one** way in which he could increase the time period of the pendulum.

....

Top Tips: In the exam, you might be expected to look at an object and describe how its design affects its stability. You're always looking for the same sort of things though — where its centre of mass is and how wide its base is. My massive bottom means I'm fairly stable and very difficult to topple.

Hydraulics

Q1 Fill in the blanks in the following passage, using the words supplied.

transmitted	force	equally	incompressible	pressure	flow

Liquids can .... and are virtually .... These properties mean that a .... exerted at one point on a liquid will be .... to other points in the liquid. .... can also be transmitted through a liquid — it is transmitted .... in all directions.

Q2 The diagram on the right shows a **simple hydraulic system**.

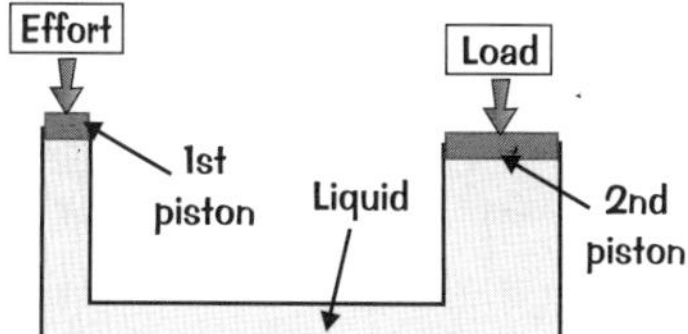

a) Hydraulic systems are used as '**force multipliers**'.
Briefly describe how a hydraulic system works as a 'force multiplier'.

piston 1 has a small surface area. pressure is placed on piston 1 which is equally transmitted through the liquid. This small force is trasmitted to the 2nd piston which has a larger surface area therefore the force is larger.

b) A force of 650 N is applied to the 1st piston, which has a cross-sectional area of 0.0025 m^2.

i) Calculate the pressure created in the liquid by the first piston.

$\frac{650}{0.0025}$ = 260000 N/m^2

ii) What will the pressure of the liquid at the 2nd piston be? Explain your answer.

260000N/m^2 because the pressure is equally transmitted throughout the liquid.

Q3 The diagram below shows two syringes connected by a tube. The entire system is filled with water. When a **force** is applied to one syringe, water passes through the tube to the other syringe.

A force of 18 N is applied to the piston of the small syringe.

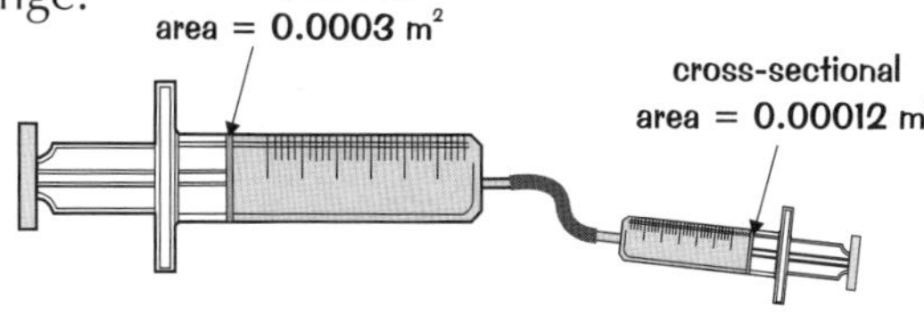

a) Calculate the pressure created by the force.

$\frac{18}{0.00012}$ = 150000 N/m^2

b) Calculate the force acting on the piston of the larger syringe.

150000 × 0.0003 = 45 N

Circular Motion

Q1 Which of the following is the **best explanation** of acceleration? Circle the appropriate letter.

A an increase in speed
B a change in direction
C an increase in velocity
D a change in velocity
E a change in speed

Q2 The diagram below shows a clock with hands that move **steadily** around the clock-face.

a) Draw and label with 'A' an arrow on the diagram to show the direction of the **velocity** of the tip of the **minute hand**.

b) Draw and label with 'B' an arrow to show the direction of the **acceleration** of the tip of the **hour hand**.

Q3 A **satellite** orbiting the Earth travels at a constant speed.

a) Is the satellite accelerating? Explain your answer.

....

b) Put a tick next to each true statement below.

☐ "If a body is accelerating then there must be a resultant force acting on it."

☐ "The forces acting on a body going round in a circle at a steady speed must be balanced."

☐ "If there is no resultant force acting on a body then it carries on moving in a straight line at the same speed."

c) What is the general name for a force that keeps a body moving in a circular path?

....

d) Draw lines to match up the following bodies with the force that keeps them moving in a circle.

A runner running round a circular track	Gravity
A satellite in orbit round the Earth	Tension
The seats at the ends of the spokes of a spinning fairground ride	Friction

Q4 Circle the correct options in these sentences.

a) The greater the mass of a body, the **smaller** / **greater** the force needed to keep it moving in a circle.

b) The faster the speed of a body, the **smaller** / **greater** the force needed to keep it moving in a circle.

c) A cyclist rides round a circular track at a speed of 20 m/s.
The frictional force between his tyres and the track is 1467 N.
He speeds up to 21 m/s — the frictional force changes to **1617 N** / **1331 N**.

Magnetic Fields

Q1 Which **one** of the following statements is correct? Tick the box next to the correct statement.

- ☐ Magnetic fields can only be detected by another magnetic device such as a compass.
- ☐ Items made from iron, aluminium and steel are all attracted to a magnet.
- ☐ Magnetic fields can exert a force on a wire carrying a current.
- ☐ The magnetic field created around a current-carrying wire points in the same direction as the flow of current through the wire.

Q2 The diagram below shows a wire carrying a current passing through a piece of flat card.

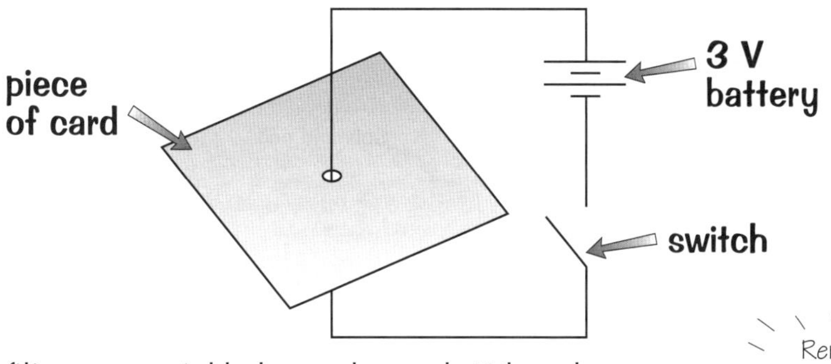

piece of card

3 V battery

switch

Some iron filings are sprinkled onto the card. When the current is switched on, a pattern develops in the iron filings.

On the diagram, sketch the pattern which the iron filings make, including arrows to show the direction of the magnetic field.

Remember the direction of conventional current flow. Then use the Right-Hand Thumb Rule.

Q3 The diagram below shows a coil of wire (a solenoid) carrying a current.

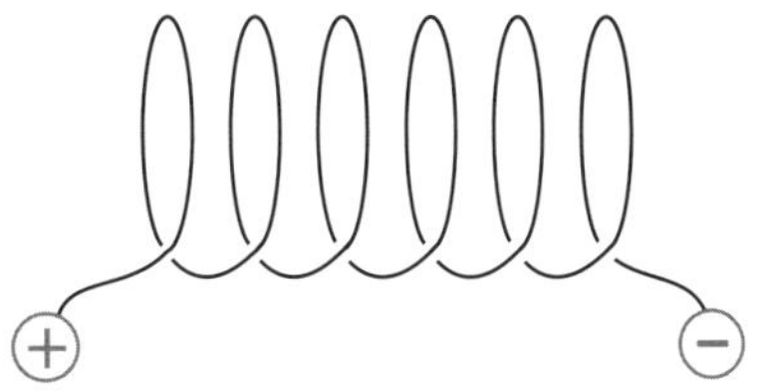

+ −

a) Draw the shape of the magnetic field around the coil.

b) What effect would the solenoid have on a piece of soft iron placed near one of its ends?

....

....

c) A soft iron core is placed in the middle of the coil. The core becomes magnetised when a current flows through the wire, and loses its magnetism when the current is switched off.

What is the name of this type of magnet?

....

Magnetic Fields

Q4 Electromagnets are often found in cranes used for lifting iron and steel.
Explain why electromagnets are **more useful** than ordinary magnets for this purpose.

Q5 The diagram shows how a solenoid can be used as a relay to switch an external circuit on and off.

To external circuit (230 V)
Solenoid coil
Soft iron core
Metal contacts
Springy metal
Switch
Low voltage DC source
To external circuit (230 V)

a) Describe what happens when the switch is closed and then opened again.

b) Give two reasons why a **soft iron** core is used in the solenoid.

Top Tips: Only **iron**, **steel** (which contains iron), **nickel** and **cobalt** are magnetic. Other metals won't stick to magnets. That's why you sometimes get magnets next to aluminium recycling bins — if a can sticks to the magnet, you know it's **not** aluminium.

The Motor Effect

Q1 Complete the passage below using the words supplied.

~~force~~ ~~angle~~ ~~stronger~~ ~~current~~ ~~magnetic field~~ ~~motor~~ ~~permanent magnets~~
A wire carrying an electric current has a ...magnetic... ...field... around it. This can interact with the magnetic fields of other wires or of ...permanent... ...magnets... to produce a ...force... and sometimes movement. A bigger ...current... or a ...stronger... magnet will produce a bigger force. The size of the force will also depend on the ...angle... at which the two magnetic fields meet each other. A force is experienced by a current-carrying wire in a magnetic field — this is known as the ...motor... effect.

Q2 The diagram shows an electrical wire between two magnetic poles. When the current is switched on, the wire moves at right angles to the magnetic field.

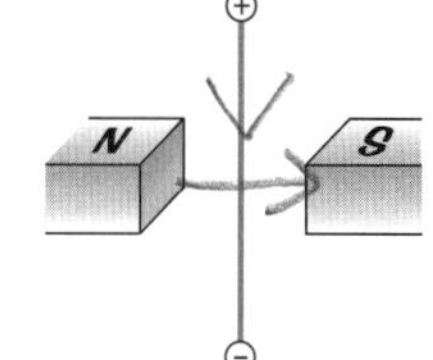

a) Using Fleming's Left-Hand Rule, state which way the wire will move.

come out towards me

b) How could the wire be made to move in the opposite direction?

Swap the magnets around.

Q3 Read the three statements below. Tick the box next to each statement that you think is **true**.

- [ ] A current-carrying wire will not experience a force if it is parallel to the magnetic field of a permanent magnet.
- [x] A current-carrying wire will not experience a force if it is at right-angles to the magnetic field of a permanent magnet.
- [ ] A current-carrying wire will not experience a force if it is at an angle of 45° to the magnetic field of a permanent magnet.

Q4 The diagram shows an aerial view of a copper wire carrying a current down into the page.

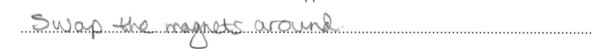

Electrical wire with insulated copper core

N S

State which way the wire will move.

~~come out towards me~~ will come out towards me

The Simple Electric Motor

Q1 Which of the following will **not** make an electric motor spin faster? Tick **one** of the boxes.

- [ ] Using a stronger magnetic field.
- [ ] Using a bigger current.
- [x] Using a commutator.

Q2 Read the three statements below. Tick the box next to each statement that you think is **true**.

- [ ] The split-ring commutator increases the size of the electric current.
- [x] The split-ring commutator reverses the direction of the current every half turn by swapping the contacts to the DC supply.
- [ ] The split-ring commutator makes the motor rotate in a different direction.

Q3 Suggest two ways in which the direction of spin of a simple DC motor can be reversed.

swapping the magnets / reverse the magnetic field

Q4 The electric motor is often used in lifts in tall buildings and mines.
Describe briefly how an electric motor can be used to raise (and lower) a lift cage.

The motor can move anticlockwise and clockwise, because of the direction of the force, this could raise the cage and lower it.
The magnetic field or current reverses when lifting the cage.

Q5 Fill in the blanks, using the words below, to explain how a **loudspeaker** works. Use the **diagram** of a loudspeaker to the right to help you.

Coil of wire
Cone
Vibration
Magnet
AC from amplifier

move	amplifier	force	field
sound	magnetic	frequency	current

The loudspeaker relies on the fact that a wire carrying a ...current... in a ...magnetic... ...field... can experience a ...force... . A coil is attached to a cardboard or plastic cone. An AC signal is then sent to the coil from an ...amplifier... . This makes the coil ...move... and causes the cone to vibrate. The cone vibrates at the same ...frequency... as the signal from the amplifier and produces ...sound... .

Electromagnetic Induction

Q1 The apparatus in the diagram below can be used to demonstrate electromagnetic induction.

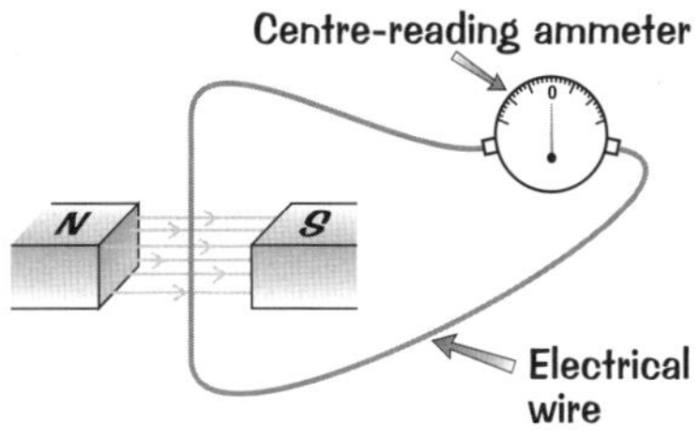

a) What is electromagnetic induction?

....

....

....

b) Describe how you could use the apparatus to demonstrate electromagnetic induction.

....

....

c) What would you see on the ammeter?

....

d) What effect would swapping the magnets have?

....

Q2 Moving a magnet inside an electric coil produces a trace on a cathode ray oscilloscope.

When the magnet was pushed **inside** the coil, **trace A** was produced on the screen.

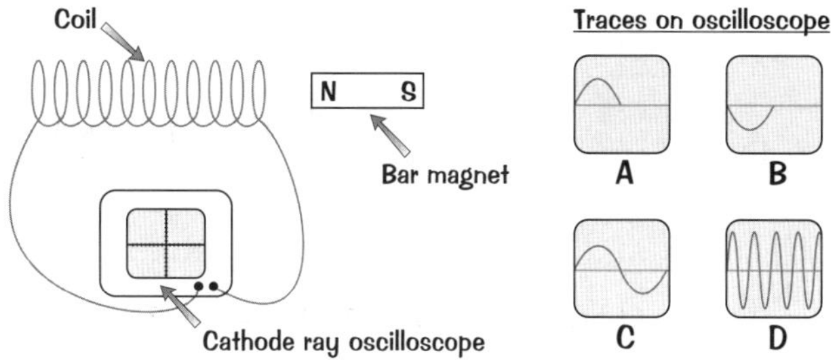

a) Explain how trace B could be produced.

....

....

b) Explain how trace C could be produced.

....

c) Explain how trace D could be produced.

....

Q3 To the right is a diagram of a **dynamo** used to power lights on a bicycle.
Use the diagram to help you explain **how** a dynamo works.

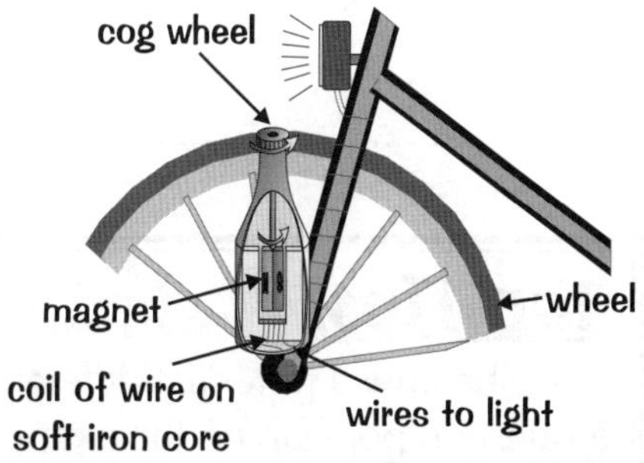

....

....

....

....

Transformers

Q1 The sentences below describe how a **transformer** works but are in the wrong order. Number the boxes 1 to 5 to show the correct order.

- ☐ The magnetic field produced inside the secondary coil induces an alternating potential difference at the ends of the secondary coil.
- ☐ This produces an alternating magnetic field in the iron core.
- ☐ An alternating current flows in the primary coil.
- ☐ If this is applied to an external circuit, an alternating current will flow in that circuit.
- ☐ A source of alternating potential difference is applied to the primary coil.

Q2 Look at the diagram to the right showing two electrical circuits.

Left coil

Right coil

Centre-reading ammeter

When the switch is closed, a deflection is seen on the ammeter and then the needle returns to zero. When the switch is opened again, a deflection is seen in the opposite direction.

a) Explain why this happens.

....

....

....

b) What could you add to the apparatus to make the needle move further?

....

Q3 Tick the boxes to indicate whether the following statements are **true** or **false**.

	True	False
Step-down transformers have fewer turns on the secondary coil than the primary coil.	☐	☐
If you put a DC into the primary coil, a DC will be produced in the secondary coil.	☐	☐
When a transformer is operating it behaves as though a bar magnet was being pushed into and pulled out of the secondary coil.	☐	☐

Q4 Many household electrical goods such as computers and radios need a lower voltage than the 230 V mains voltage. What sort of transformer is used to reduce the voltage for these goods?

....

Top Tips: It can be a bit tricky remembering how a transformer works — make sure you can describe **how** a potential difference is induced in the **secondary coil**. Not only will it be useful in case a question pops up on the exam, but it's also a great icebreaker topic when meeting new people.

Transformers

Q5 The following statements are **false**. Below each statement, write a correct version.

a) A transformer consists of an iron core and one wire coil.

....

b) Step-up transformers have more turns on the primary coil than the secondary coil.

....

....

c) In a step-down transformer the potential difference across the secondary coil is greater than the potential difference across the primary coil.

....

....

....

Derek's transformation didn't go quite as he'd planned.

Q6 Transformers have an **iron core**.

a) Explain why a potential difference is induced in the **secondary coil** when an alternating current flows in the primary coil.

....

....

b) Why do transformers work with **alternating** current **only**?

....

....

Q7 Ash is discussing transformers with his friends. He says:

"The core of a transformer has to be made of a conducting material such as iron so the current can get through."

Is Ash right or wrong? Give a reason for your answer.

Ash is .... because ....

....

Transformers

Q8 Many modern appliances use **switch mode transformers**.

a) Tick the boxes to show whether the following statements about switch mode transformers are **true** or **false**.

	True	False
They usually operate at a frequency between 50 kHz and 200 kHz.	☐	☐
They're usually smaller and lighter than traditional transformers.	☐	☐
They operate at lower frequencies than traditional transformers.	☐	☐
They use very little power when they're switched on and no load is applied.	☐	☐

b) Name **one** device that uses a switch mode transformer.

....

Q9 Tim is investigating a transformer. He uses it to power a **spotlight**, and measures the **voltage** and **current** for both the **primary** and **secondary coils**. Here are his results.

Voltage to primary coil (V)	Current in primary coil (A)	Voltage to secondary coil (V)	Current in secondary coil (A)
240	0.25	12	5.0

a) Is Tim's transformer a **step-up** or **step-down** transformer? Give a reason for your answer.

....

....

b) i) Calculate the power in the **primary** coil when using the spotlight.

....

....

ii) Calculate the power in the **secondary** coil when using the spotlight.

....

....

c) What idea about the **efficiency** of a transformer is confirmed by Tim's results?

....

Top Tips: Crikey, you should know transformers inside and out after all those wonderful questions... and there's another juicy page of questions still to come. Make sure you can rearrange the transformer equations with ease and know the advantages of switch mode transformers too.

Transformers

Q10 A transformer has 100 turns in its primary coil and 4000 turns in its secondary coil. What input voltage would produce an output voltage of 10 000 V?

....

....

Q11 Use the **transformer equation** to complete the following table.

Number of turns on primary coil	Voltage to primary coil (V)	Number of turns on secondary coil	Voltage to secondary coil (V)
1000	12	4000	
1000		2000	20
1000	12		12
	33 000	500	230

Q12 A transformer has **5000** turns on its **primary** coil and **8000** turns on its **secondary** coil.

a) If the input voltage is 230 V, find the output voltage.

....

b) Andy has built a radio which needs a 20 V electricity supply. The mains supply to Andy's house is 230 V. How could Andy adapt the transformer described above to make it suitable for his radio?

....

....

....

....

Q13 A transformer in an adaptor is used to **step down** a **230 V** mains electricity supply to the **110 V** needed for an electric fan heater.

Calculate the current drawn by the transformer from the mains supply, if the current through the heater is **20 A**. Assume that the transformer is 100% efficient.

....

....

Mixed Questions — Physics 3b

Q1 Point P marks the pivot point on the wheelbarrow.

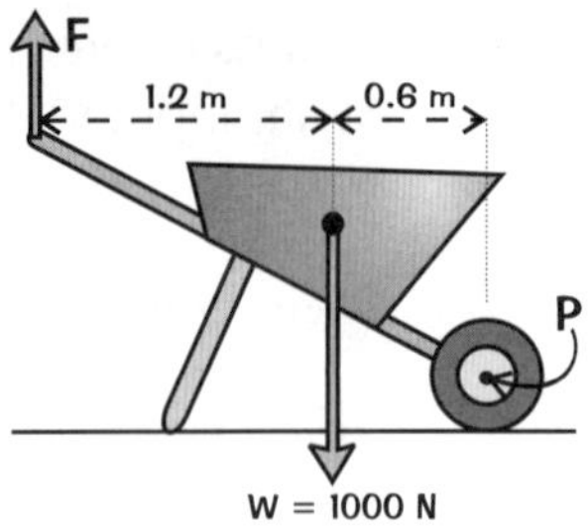

a) Take moments about P to find the **vertical** force, F, that needs to be applied to the handles of the wheelbarrow to just lift it off the ground.

....

....

b) The wheelbarrow tipped over while it was being pushed, fully loaded, across some rocky ground. Explain why this happened using the phrases **resultant moment** and **centre of mass** in your answer.

....

....

c) Write down **two** factors which affect the stability of an object.

1. ....

2. ....

Q2 Mick takes his younger brother Huck on a trip to a fairground.

a) They decide to go on the swinging pirate ship first. If the time period of each swing of the ship is **2 seconds**, calculate the **frequency** of the ship.

....

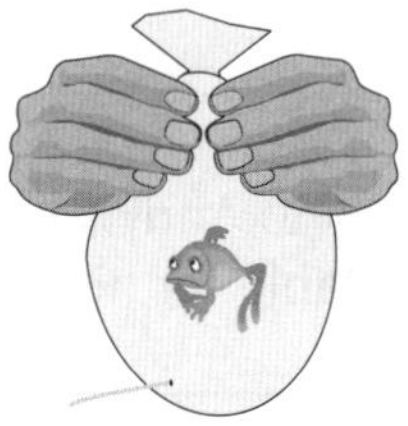

b) Mick wins a goldfish on a fairground stall. When he squeezes the top of bag, water squirts out of a hole at the bottom. Explain briefly, in terms of **forces**, why this happens.

....

....

c) Mick decides to try out the "Test Your Strength!" game.

The game works using a **simple hydraulic system** (see right). Mick uses a wooden mallet to hit a small piston.

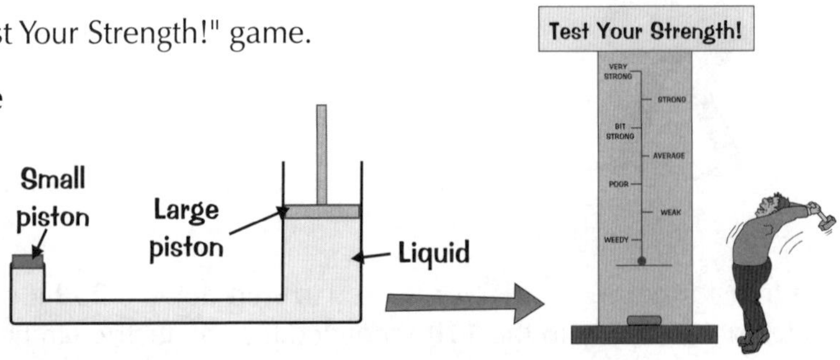

Use the diagram to explain why the **upwards** force at the larger piston will be **greater** than the force of the mallet on the smaller piston.

....

....

....

Mixed Questions — Physics 3b

Q3 The diagram below shows how an **electromagnet** can be used to switch on a car's starter motor.

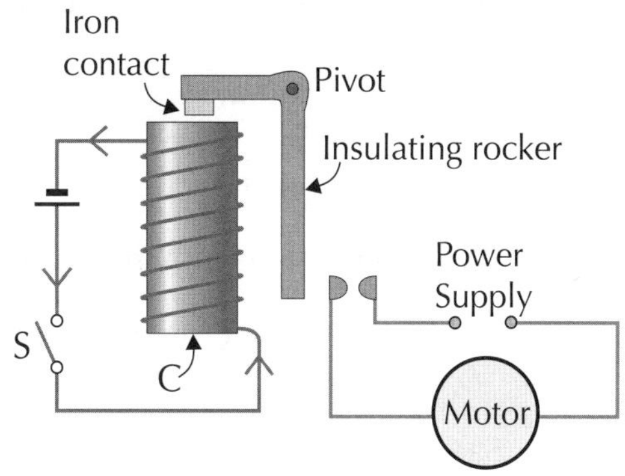

a) What is the function of the iron core, C?

....

....

b) Describe what happens when the switch, S, is closed.

....

....

....

....

Q4 The diagram below shows a simple **motor**. The coil is rotating as shown.

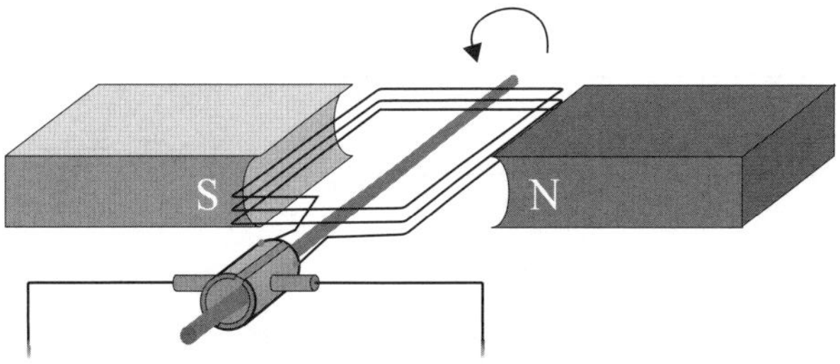

a) On the diagram, draw arrows labelled 'F' to show the direction of the **force** on each arm of the coil.

b) Draw arrows labelled 'I' on each arm of the coil to show the direction the **current** is flowing.

c) State two ways of increasing the **speed** of this motor.

1...

2...

Q5 The diagram shows a **bicycle dynamo**.

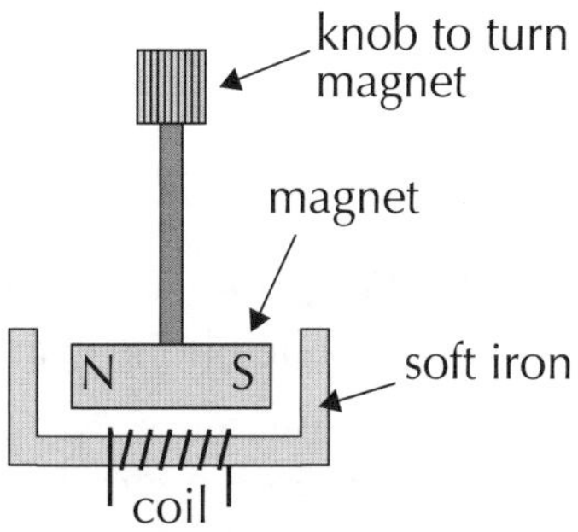

a) What happens in the coil of wire when the knob is rotated **clockwise** at a constant speed? Explain your answer.

....

....

....

b) What would change if the magnet were rotated **anticlockwise** (at the same speed as before)?

....

Mixed Questions — Physics 3b

Q6 TV satellite **A** shown below orbits the Earth at a distance of 35 800 km above the surface.

a) What provides the centripetal force that keeps the satellite moving in a circular path?

....

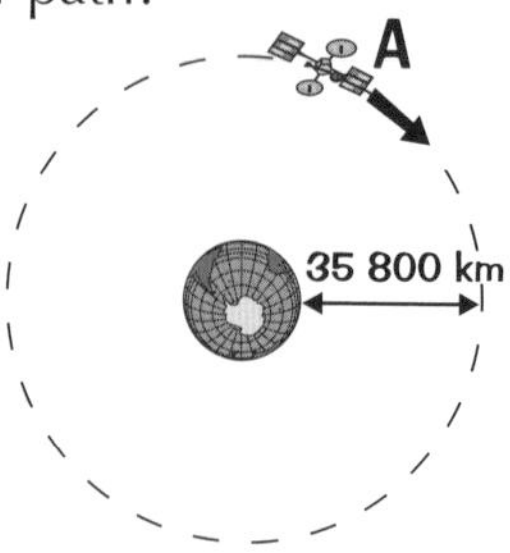

b) Indicate whether each of these statements is true or false.

	True	False
i) The satellite is moving at a constant velocity.	☐	☐
ii) The centripetal force acts away from the centre of the circle.	☐	☐

c) Satellite B has the same mass as satellite A and is in orbit 40 000 km above the Earth.

Which satellite, A or B, has the greatest centripetal force acting on it? ....

Q7 The diagram shows a traditional **transformer**.

a) What is the output voltage, V?

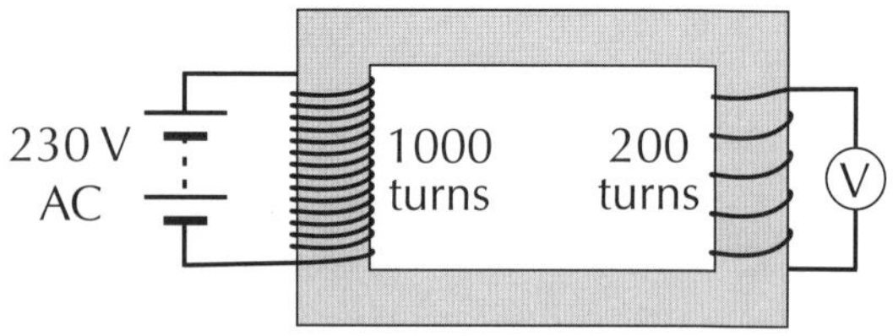

....

....

....

b) Transformers are usually wound on a **core**.

i) Name the metal used for the core of the transformer. ....

ii) Why is the core a necessary part of a transformer?

....

....

c) A different transformer is needed to 'step down' a power supply from 33 kV to 230 V.
It has 2000 turns on its primary coil. How many turns should it have on its secondary coil?

....

....

d) Describe the advantages of using a **switch mode transformer** in a mobile phone charger, compared to a traditional transformer.

....

....

....

SAEW44